Letts GCSE Success

Revision Guide

AQA Science Higher

Brian Arnold • Hannah Kingston • Emma Poole

Contents

Biology

	Revised
The nervous system ... 4	☐
The reflex arc ... 6	☐
The menstrual cycle ... 8	☐
A balanced diet ... 10	☐
Nutrition and health ... 12	☐
Causes of disease ... 14	☐
Defence against disease ... 16	☐
Treatment of disease ... 18	☐
Drugs ... 20	☐
Genetic engineering ... 22	☐
Genes ... 24	☐
Selective breeding ... 26	☐
Evolution ... 28	☐
Evidence for evolution ... 30	☐
Adaptation and competition ... 32	☐
Environmental damage ... 34	☐
Practice questions ... 36	☐

Chemistry

	Revised
Atoms and elements ... 38	☐
Limestone ... 40	☐
Fuels ... 42	☐
Organic families ... 44	☐
Vegetable oils ... 46	☐
Plastics ... 48	☐
Ethanol ... 50	☐
Evolution of the atmosphere ... 52	☐
Pollution of the atmosphere ... 54	☐

	Revised
Pollution of the environment	56 ☐
Evidence for plate tectonics	58 ☐
Consequences of plate tectonics	60 ☐
Extraction of iron	62 ☐
Iron and steel	64 ☐
Aluminium	66 ☐
Titanium and copper	68 ☐
Transition metals	70 ☐
The noble gases	72 ☐
Practice questions	74 ☐

Physics

	Revised
Energy	76 ☐
Efficiency	78 ☐
Generating electricity	80 ☐
Renewable sources of energy	82 ☐
Heat transfer – conduction	84 ☐
Heat transfer – convection	86 ☐
Heat transfer – radiation	88 ☐
Electrical power	90 ☐
Radiation/Waves	92 ☐
The electromagnetic spectrum	94 ☐
Analogue and digital signals	96 ☐
Nuclear radiation	98 ☐
Radioactivity and half life	100 ☐
Uses of radioactivity	102 ☐
Our universe	104 ☐
Exploring space	106 ☐
Practice questions	108 ☐

Answers 110

The nervous system

The nervous system is in charge! It *controls and co-ordinates* the parts of your body so that they work together at the right time.

The nervous system co-ordinates things you don't even think about, like breathing and blinking.

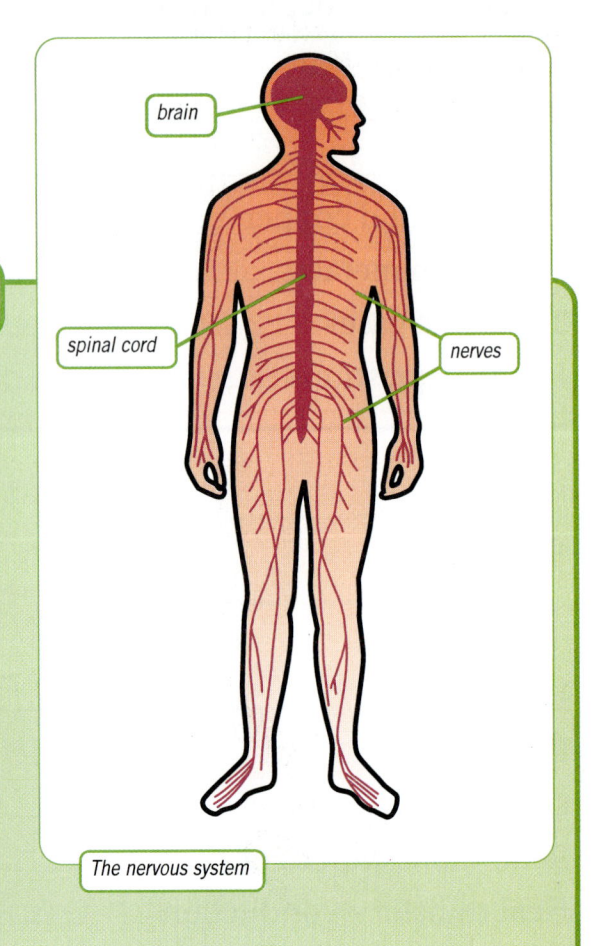

The central nervous system

The central nervous system (CNS) consists of the brain and the spinal cord connected to different parts of the body by **nerves**.

Your body's sense organs contain receptors.

Receptors detect changes in the environment called stimuli.

The receptors send messages along nerves to the brain and spinal cord in response to stimuli from the environment.

The messages are called nerve impulses.

The CNS sends nerve impulses back along nerves to effectors which bring about a response.

Effectors are muscles that bring about movement, or glands that secrete hormones.

The nervous system

Nerves

Nerves are made up of nerve cells or neurones. Neurones have a nucleus, cytoplasm, and cell membrane, but they have changed their shape and become specialised. There are three types of neurone.

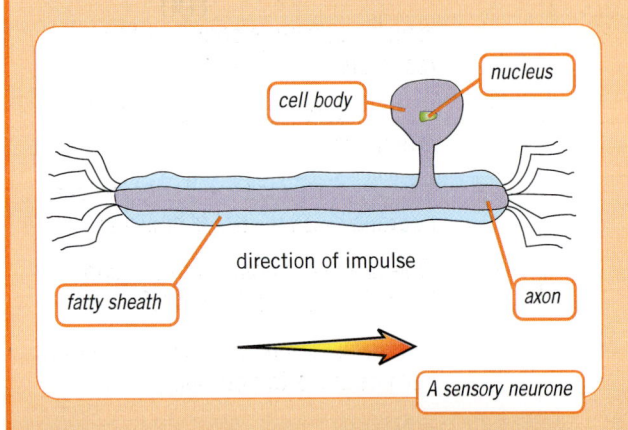

A sensory neurone

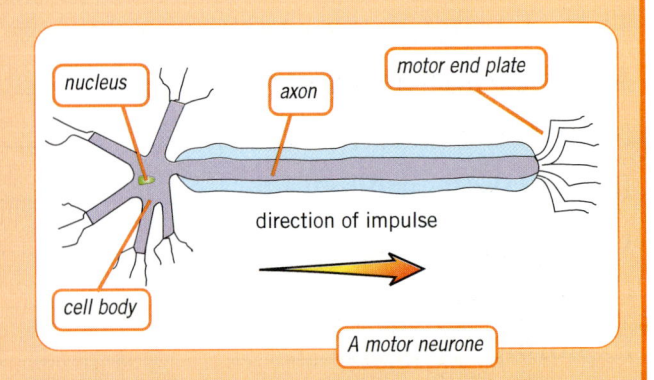

A motor neurone

The motor neurones send messages from the CNS to the effectors telling them what to do.

Nerve impulses travel in **one direction only**.

The fatty sheath is for insulation and for speeding up nerve impulses.

A relay neurone connects the sensory neurone to the motor neurone in the CNS.

The sensory neurones receive messages from the receptors and send them to the CNS.

Synapses

In between the neurones there is a gap called a **synapse**.

- When an impulse reaches the end of an axon a chemical is released.
- This chemical diffuses across the gap.
- This starts off an impulse in the next neurone.

Synapses can be affected by drugs and alcohol, slowing down synapses or even stopping them.

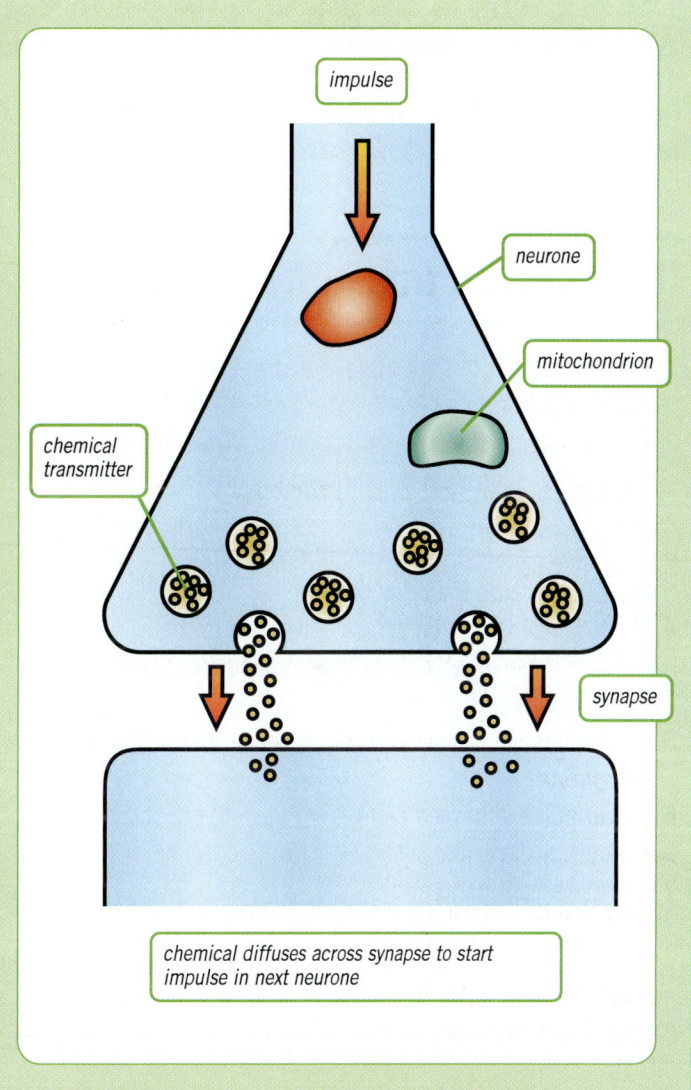

impulse

neurone

mitochondrion

chemical transmitter

synapse

chemical diffuses across synapse to start impulse in next neurone

THE NERVOUS SYSTEM

Biology

KEY TERMS

Make sure you understand these terms before moving on!

- CNS
- receptors
- nerve impulses
- effectors
- sensory neurones
- motor neurones
- relay neurone
- synapse

QUICK TEST

1. Name the five sense organs.
2. What is CNS an abbreviation for?
3. What does the CNS consist of?
4. Name the three types of neurone.
5. What is a synapse?
6. Which neurone is connected to receptors?
7. Which neurone is connected to the effectors?
8. Which neurone connects the sensory neurone and the motor neurone?
9. True or false, nerve impulses can travel in one direction only?
10. How is the nerve impulse transmitted from neurone to neurone?

The reflex arc

The reflex response to your CNS and back again can be shown in a diagram called the *reflex arc*.

The reflex arc

1. The stimulus in this example is a sharp object but it could be a hot object.
2. The receptor is the pain sensor in the skin which detects the sharpness as pain and generates a nerve impulse.
3. The nerve impulse travels along the sensory neurone towards the relay neurone.
4. The impulse is passed across a synapse to the relay neurone which carries the impulse towards the motor neurone.
5. The impulse is passed across a synapse to the motor neurone.
6. The impulse is passed along a synapse to the muscle effector in the arm.
7. You move your hand away.

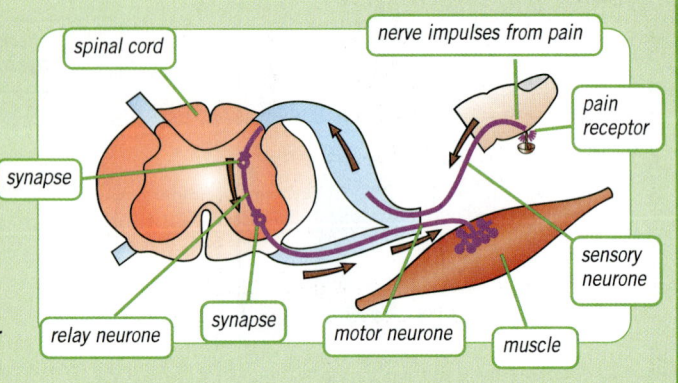

The reflex arc can be shown in a block diagram:

stimulus → receptor → sensory neurone → relay neurone → motor neurone → effector → response

Diseases of the nervous system

Multiple sclerosis is caused by the fatty sheath around the neurone breaking down. Without the fatty sheath, impulses slow down or even stop, preventing the messages reaching the muscles.

Motor neurone disease affects the neurones that join the muscles. The neurones break down and cannot transmit nerve impulses so the muscles cannot contract and the person becomes paralysed.

Reflex and voluntary actions

- **Voluntary actions** are things you have to think about, like talking and writing. They are under conscious control and they have to be learned.
- **Reflex actions** produce rapid involuntary responses and they often protect us, and other animals, from harm. Examples include reflex actions in a newborn baby, the pupils' response to light and the knee-jerk reflex. Simple reflex actions help animals survive as they respond to a **stimulus** such as smelling and finding food or avoidance of predators.

In certain circumstances the brain can override a reflex response. For example, the brain sends a message to the motor neurone in the reflex arc to keep hold of that hot plate and not to drop it.

A reflex response to a new situation can be learned, this is called **conditioning** and involves a secondary stimulus. For example, the smell of food makes dogs produce saliva. Pavlov, a scientist, introduced a bell instead of a smell that also triggered saliva production.

Homeostasis

The nervous system and hormones enable us to respond to **external changes in the environment** by **monitoring and changing our internal environment**. Our internal environment changes very little and stays at a safe level; this is called **homeostasis**. This is all under the control of nerves and hormones.

Internal conditions which are controlled include:

- The water content of the body, we drink to replace water lost in sweating and breathing. Excess water is lost in urine.
- The ion content of the body, we lose ions such as salt when we sweat. Excess ions are lost in the urine.
- The temperature of the body needs to be maintained to enable enzymes to work effectively.
- Blood sugar levels are monitored by hormones so that the cells receive a constant supply of energy.

Make sure you learn the diagram of the reflex arc and the block diagram, either one may come up in the exam.

Learn examples that follow the reflex arc, for example touching a hot object or dust in the eye.

KEY TERMS

Make sure you understand these terms before moving on!

- reflex arc
- multiple sclerosis
- motor neurone disease
- voluntary action
- reflex action
- stimulus
- conditioning
- homeostasis

QUICK TEST

1. Where in your body might you find a relay neurone?
2. How many synapses are there in a typical reflex arc?
3. What has to happen first before a reflex arc can take place?
4. Is blinking a reflex action?
5. Why do we have reflex actions?
6. What is the difference between a reflex action and a voluntary action?
7. Do you think you can stop reflex actions? Try to name a situation.
8. Which comes first in a reflex arc, the receptor or the effector?
9. Which neurone passes the nerve impulse to the effector?
10. Which neurone receives the nerve impulse from the receptor?

THE REFLEX ARC

Biology

The menstrual cycle

Hormones are chemicals released from glands in the body straight into the blood stream to the target organs. The effects of hormones are slower than nervous messages but are longer lasting. Hormones control things that need constant adjustment. An example is the menstrual cycle in women where several hormones are involved.

The menstrual cycle

The 28-day menstrual cycle

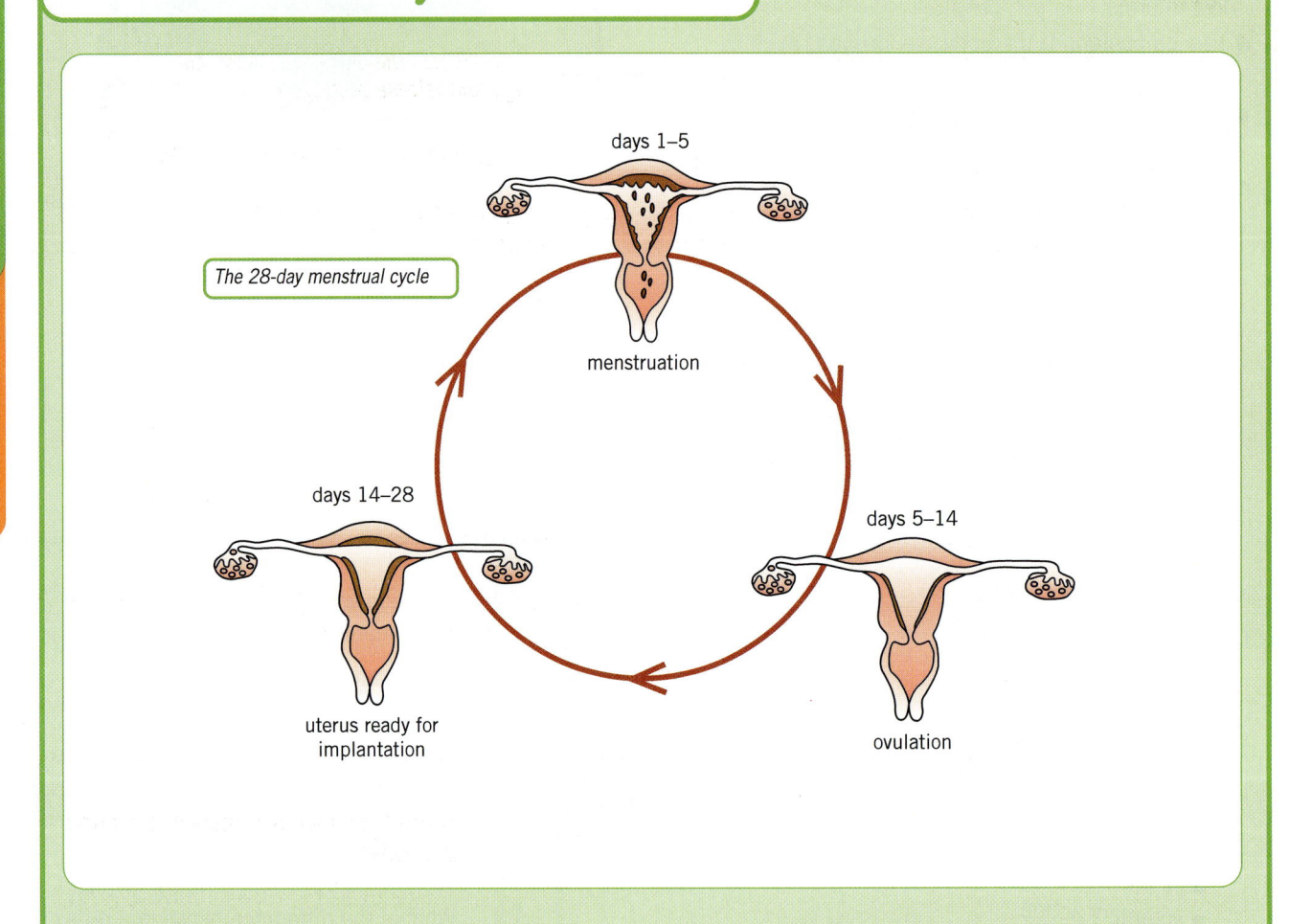

- days 1–5 — menstruation
- days 5–14 — ovulation
- days 14–28 — uterus ready for implantation

The menstrual cycle lasts approximately **28 days**.

It consists of a **menstrual bleed and ovulation** – the release of an egg.

Hormones control the whole cycle.

The ovaries secrete the hormones **progesterone** and **oestrogen**.

The stages of the menstrual cycle

Days 1–5 a menstrual bleed (a period) occurs and the lining of the uterus breaks down. This is caused by a **lack of progesterone**.

Days 5–14 oestrogen is released from the ovaries and the uterus lining builds up again. Oestrogen also stimulates egg development and release of the egg from the ovaries – called **ovulation**.

Days 14–28 progesterone is released which maintains the uterus lining. If no fertilisation occurs then progesterone production stops.

Days 28–5 cycle begins again.

The pituitary gland

The two hormones released from the ovaries are in fact controlled by the **pituitary gland** situated at the base of the brain.

The pituitary gland secretes two more hormones; follicle stimulating hormone and luteinising hormone. There is no need to learn how to spell them as they can be written as **FSH** and **LH**.

The diagram shows how the hormones interact to control the menstrual cycle.

- **Progesterone** is released which maintains the uterus lining.
- **Oestrogen** also keeps the uterus lining thick ready for pregnancy.
- If no pregnancy occurs then progesterone production stops and the cycle begins again.

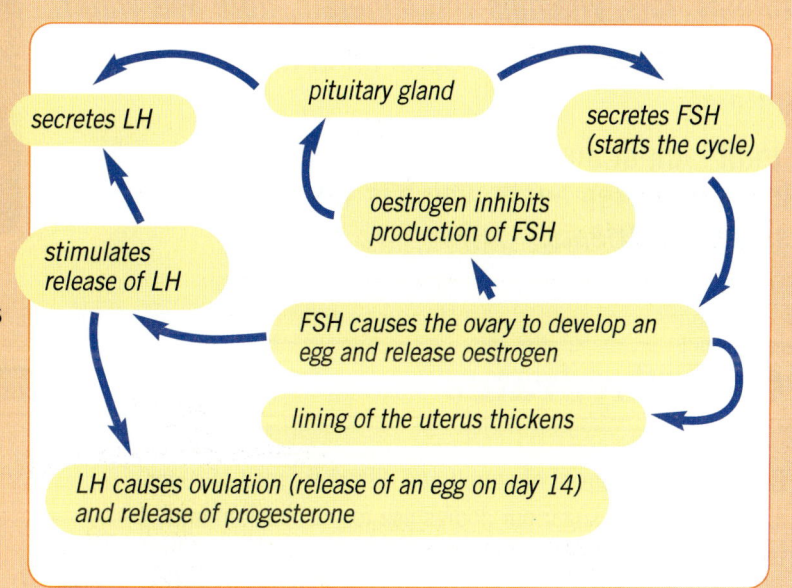

Diagram flow:
- pituitary gland secretes FSH (starts the cycle)
- FSH causes the ovary to develop an egg and release oestrogen
- oestrogen inhibits production of FSH
- lining of the uterus thickens
- stimulates release of LH
- secretes LH
- LH causes ovulation (release of an egg on day 14) and release of progesterone

Controlling fertility

Fertility in women can be controlled in two ways:

- FSH can be administered as a '**fertility drug**' to women whose own production is too low to stimulate eggs to mature. This can result in multiple births.
- Oestrogen can be used as an **oral contraceptive** to inhibit FSH so that no eggs mature.

IVF

In vitro fertilisation (**IVF**) is a treatment for infertile couples. It involves extracting the eggs and sperm and fertilising them outside the body. The cells that develop are then implanted in the womb for growth and development into an embryo.

FSH is the hormone used to stimulate egg production.

💡 *Be prepared to evaluate the benefits and problems associated with the use of hormones to control fertility. For example, do they interfere with nature? Or are the possible side effects they may cause a risk worth taking?*

💡 *The role of the hormones in controlling the menstrual cycle is a favourite for the exam.*

KEY TERMS

- hormones
- progesterone
- oestrogen
- ovulation
- pituitary gland
- FSH
- LH
- fertility drug
- IVF

QUICK TEST

1. How are hormones transported around the body?
2. What causes the uterus lining to break down?
3. Where are the hormones oestrogen and progesterone made?
4. From where are the eggs released?
5. Which hormone is used in IVF?
6. Which two hormones are produced by the pituitary gland?
7. What two things does follicle stimulating hormone do?
8. Which two hormones maintain the uterus lining?
9. What is ovulation?
10. What is IVF an abbreviation for?

A balanced diet

The seven nutritional groups are: *carbohydrates, proteins, fats, vitamins* and *minerals, fibre* and *water*.

A balanced diet is made up of all of the seven nutrients.

A total lack of any one important nutrient will cause illness and even death which is why they are called *essential nutrients*.

Carbohydrates

Carbohydrates consist of starch and different types of sugar, e.g. glucose (the sugar our bodies use for respiration) and lactose (the sugar in milk).

We need carbohydrates to **give us energy**.

Starch is actually made up of smaller glucose molecules joined together. Plants store glucose as starch.

Glycogen is also a carbohydrate. Animals store glucose as glycogen.

proteins, fats, fibre

water, carbohydrates, vitamins and minerals

A balanced diet

These foods contain a lot of carbohydrate

Protein

Your body cells are made of mostly protein.

Proteins are made up of lots of amino acids.

We need protein to **repair and replace damaged cells** or to **make new cells during growth**.

These foods contain a lot of protein

Fats

Fats are made from fatty acids and glycerol.

We need fats for a **store of energy**, to **make cell membranes** and for **warmth** (**insulation**).

Fat can also be bad for us. **Cholesterol** is a fatty deposit that can narrow the arteries and can contribute to heart disease.

These foods contain a lot of fat

Biology — A BALANCED DIET

10

Fibre

Fibre or roughage comes from plants.

Fibre is not actually digested, it just keeps food moving smoothly through your system.

Fibre provides something for your gut muscles to push against. It's a bit like squeezing toothpaste through a tube.

It prevents constipation.

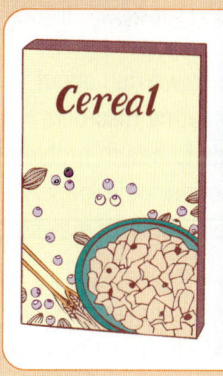

These foods contain a lot of fibre

Vitamins and minerals

We only need these in small amounts but they are essential for good health.

Your body turns everything you eat into body tissue by billions of reactions that occur in your body. Vitamins and minerals are essential to this process. They also make up cells and tissue in your body.

Vitamins and minerals are found in fruit, vegetables and cereals.

> *Remember that carbohydrates are for energy, proteins are for growth and repair and fats are for energy store and insulation. However, do not forget the other important food groups.*

Water

Water makes up approximately 65% of your body weight.

Water is important because:
- Our blood plasma is mainly water.
- Water is in sweat that cools us down.
- Chemical reactions in our cells take place in water.
- Waste products are removed from our bodies in water.

Both food and drink contain water.

KEY TERMS

Make sure you understand these terms before moving on!
- carbohydrates
- proteins
- fats
- vitamins
- minerals
- fibre
- water
- energy
- repair
- growth
- insulation

QUICK TEST

1. What do we use carbohydrates for?
2. Name the two main carbohydrates.
3. What type of carbohydrate would long distance runners need to eat before a race?
4. In cold countries, what nutritional group is particularly important?
5. Why do we need fat in our diets?
6. Why is protein important to our cells?
7. How does fibre prevent constipation?
8. When animals eat glucose they use some for energy and store some as?
9. Which food groups are only needed in small amounts?
10. What type of fat contributes to heart disease?

A BALANCED DIET — Biology

Nutrition and health

A combination of a balanced diet and exercise is needed to keep the body healthy.

A healthy diet

A healthy diet contains the right balance of the different foods you need and the right amount of energy.

The amount of energy a person needs in their diet depends on **age, gender and amount of activity**.

If a person becomes overweight then they are more likely to suffer health problems such as arthritis, diabetes, heart disease, high blood pressure, stress and anxiety.

Occasionally a person can become so worried about being overweight they can develop eating disorders such as **anorexia nervosa**. This leads to health problems such as reduced resistance to infection, pale, papery skin and, in women, irregular periods (or they may stop altogether).

In the developing world, lack of food is linked to health problems such as reduced resistance to infection from diseases.

Deficiencies

Deficiency diseases are caused by lack of vitamins and minerals, or any other essential nutrient.

- **Vitamin C** keeps the skin strong and supple. Sailors used to suffer from scurvy until lime juice, oranges and lemons were added to their diets.
- **Vitamin D** helps the bones harden in children; without it the bones stay soft and a disease called rickets develops. Vitamin D is found in fish and eggs, exposure to sunlight also helps.
- We need the **mineral iron** for making haemoglobin and the **mineral calcium** for healthy bones and teeth.
- **Kwashiorkor** is a protein deficiency disorder that is common in developing countries because their diets consist of mainly starchy vegetables. In particular, they do not get enough animal protein which contains all the essential amino acids not made in the body.

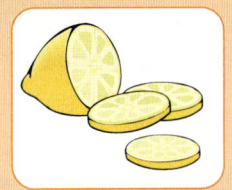

Cholesterol

Cholesterol is made in the liver and is found in the blood.

The level of cholesterol in the blood is influenced by the amount and type of fat in the diet.

Cholesterol is carried in the blood by lipoproteins. There are two types. Low-density lipoproteins (LDLs) are classed as 'bad' cholesterol and high-density lipoproteins (HDLs) are 'good' cholesterol. It is important to get the balance right to avoid heart and blood vessel disease.

Saturated fats increase blood cholesterol. Monounsaturated fats have little effect and **polyunsaturated fats** may help reduce blood cholesterol and improve the balance between LDL's and HDL's. So to keep healthy, diets need to be low in saturated fat which means avoid processed food and stick to low fat options.

Genetic factors, smoking and alcohol can also contribute to the effects of cholesterol and increase the risk of **heart disease**.

Statins are drugs that can be used to lower levels of cholesterol in the blood, they are used to treat atherosclerosis and heart disease as they reduce the formation of plaque in the arteries and also inflammation.

Metabolic rate

Metabolic rate (MR) is the rate at which your body burns calories or uses up energy to carry out all the chemical reactions that take place in your cells. Genetics affects a person's metabolic rate as well as various other factors. **Activity** increases MR and it usually stays high for some time after exercise is finished. People who exercise are usually fitter than people who don't.

The proportion of muscle to fat ratio is important. People with more muscle have a higher MR than those with more fat who have a lower MR.

Other factors that increase MR are smaller regular meals, pregnancy and cold weather (as you tend to move around more). Factors that lower MR are age (younger people have a lower rate) and crash dieting.

The Atkins diet

The Atkins diet is a slimming diet that suggests that eating a lot of protein suppresses the appetite. It suggests that you burn more calories when your body uses fat and proteins as fuel rather than carbohydrates.

The BBC2 programme Horizon used twins who study the Atkins diet. They found that the twin who was on the Atkins diet lost only 22 calories more. They concluded that there was little difference to suggest anything significant other than the fact that, without trying, the person on the diet consumed fewer calories. They also said that there was something about the diet that controls hunger.

Scientific concept

There are many health fears associated with the Atkins diet such as kidney problems, increased cholesterol and an increased risk of diabetes. It was a very popular diet but is gradually being replaced by healthy eating plans as many people only found it to be a 'quick fix' and it did not lead to long term weight loss.

Remember each individual's diet reflects their personal choice with influences such as religion and medical reasons.

Salt

Salt is needed in small amounts in our diets; an adult needs, on average, about 6 grams per day but some are actually consuming 60% more.

Too much salt in the diet has led to high blood pressure for about 30% of the population.

Salt contains sodium which is linked to heart disease, high blood pressure and strokes. It is found in high quantities in processed food, from cereals to biscuits and soups.

0.5 g of sodium in foods is considered a lot whereas 0.1 g is a little.

KEY TERMS

Make sure you understand these terms before moving on!
- cholesterol
- saturated fats
- polyunsaturated fats
- heart disease
- metabolic rate

QUICK TEST

1. If you had a diet high in saturated fats what would you be at risk of?
2. What type of fat would lower cholesterol?
3. How much salt should an average person eat per day?
4. When you read food labels, what amount of sodium is considered to be a little?
5. If a person suffers from Kwashiorkor, what are they deficient in?
6. Is a person who exercises regularly likely to have a high or low metabolic rate?
7. Where is cholesterol made?
8. What health problems are associated with being overweight?
9. How could you avoid suffering from scurvy?
10. Iron is needed to make haemoglobin which is a part of red blood cells. Who, in particular, should make sure their diet contains enough iron?

NUTRITION AND HEALTH — Biology

Causes of disease

Microbes are bacteria, fungi and viruses.

Not all microbes cause disease, some are useful.

Microbes that get inside you and make you feel ill are called *pathogens* or germs.

Pathogens rapidly reproduce in warm conditions and with plenty of food.

How are diseases spread?

- **Contact** with infected people and animals or objects used by infected people, e.g. athlete's foot, chicken pox, measles and HIV through infected blood.
- Through the **air**, e.g. flu, colds and pneumonia.
- Through infected **food and drink** e.g., cholera from infected drinking water and salmonella food poisoning.

Disease can be non infectious and caused by vitamin deficiencies such as scurvy (lack of vitamin C), mineral deficiencies such as anaemia (lack of iron) or body disorders like cancer or diabetes. Other disorders can be inherited, like red/green colour blindness or diabetes.

Bacteria

Bacteria are living organisms that feed, move and carry out respiration.

Bacteria reproduce rapidly and produce exact copies.

Bacteria are good at surviving in unfavourable conditions such as extreme temperatures. They form a protective coat around themselves and are now called **spores**.

When conditions return to normal, the bacterial cell comes out of its spore and continues to reproduce.

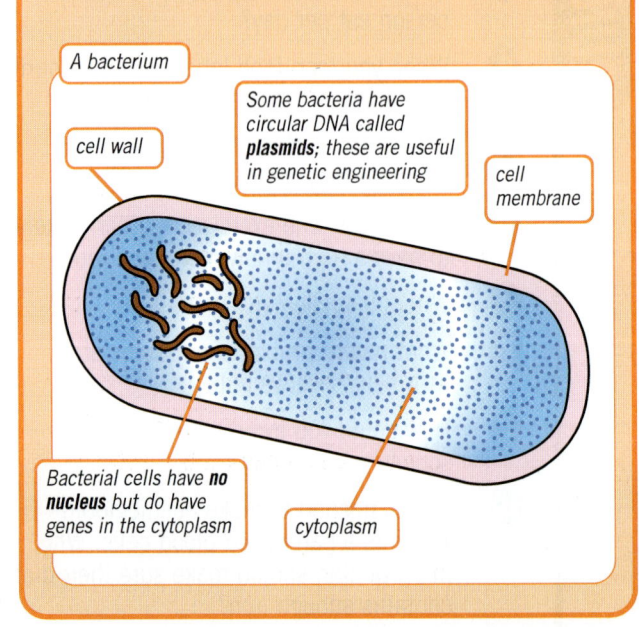

How bacteria cause disease:
- Bacteria **destroy living tissue**. For example, tuberculosis destroys lung tissue.
- Bacteria can produce poisons, called **toxins**. For example, food poisoning is caused by bacteria releasing toxins.

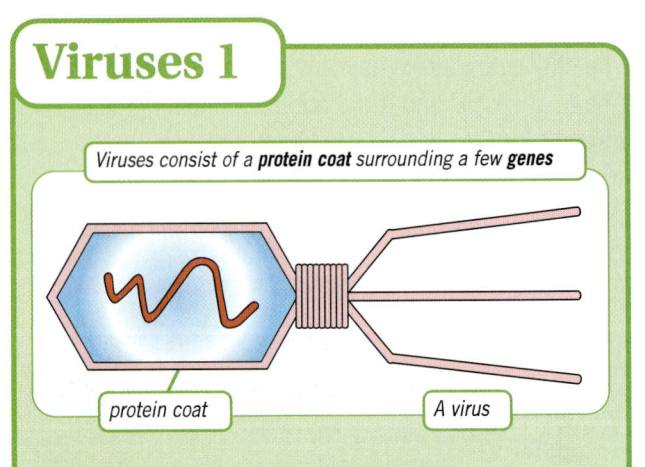

A bacterium

- cell wall
- Some bacteria have circular DNA called **plasmids**; these are useful in genetic engineering
- cell membrane
- Bacterial cells have **no nucleus** but do have genes in the cytoplasm
- cytoplasm

Viruses 1

*Viruses consist of a **protein coat** surrounding a few **genes***

- protein coat
- A virus

Viruses are much smaller than bacteria.

Viruses don't feed, move, respire or grow, they just reproduce.

Viruses can only survive inside the cells of a living organism.

Viruses 2

They **reproduce inside the cells** and release thousands of new viruses to infect new cells.

They **kill the cell** in the process.

Examples of viruses causing disease are HIV, flu, chicken pox and measles.

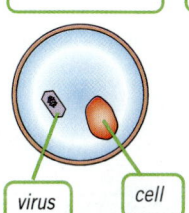

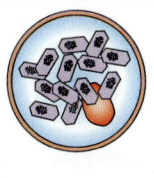

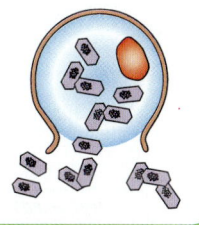

| virus enters cell | virus reproduces | cell bursts – viruses invade new cells |

virus   cell

💡 *Learn the structure of a bacterium and a virus; notice the similarities and differences between them and general animal and plant cells.*

Symptoms of infection

Symptoms are the effects diseases have on the body; the symptoms are usually caused by the toxins released by the pathogens.

Symptoms include a high temperature, headache, loss of appetite and sickness.

💡 *Remember that not all microbes are harmful and cause disease.*

Fungi

Fungi cause athlete's foot and ringworm.

Fungi reproduce by **making spores** that can be carried from person to person.

Most fungi are useful as decomposers. Yeast is a fungus that is used in bread, beer and wine making.

Vectors

Some pathogens rely on **vectors** to transfer them from one organism to another. A vector is an organism that transports a pathogen. An example would be a **mosquito**.

A mosquito that is carrying the bacteria that causes malaria from one person may infect another person by injecting the bacteria into the person's bloodstream when it bites them.

How do pathogens get in?

Pathogens have to enter our body before they can do any harm.

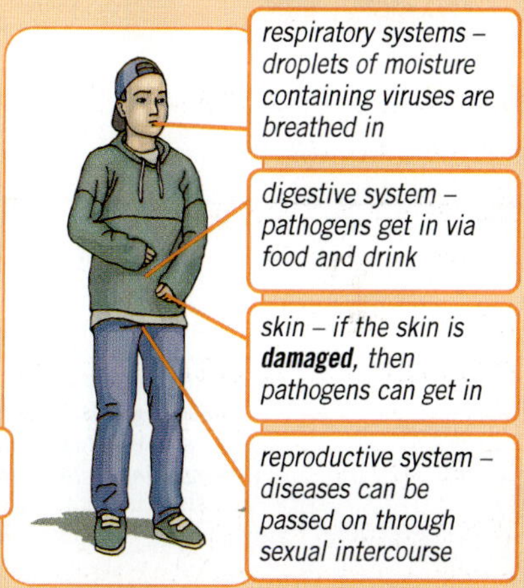

- respiratory systems – droplets of moisture containing viruses are breathed in
- digestive system – pathogens get in via food and drink
- skin – if the skin is **damaged**, then pathogens can get in
- reproductive system – diseases can be passed on through sexual intercourse

Routes for microbes to enter the body

KEY TERMS
- microbes
- viruses
- bacteria
- pathogens
- toxins
- vectors

QUICK TEST

1. Name the three types of microbes.
2. What do we call microbes that cause disease?
3. Why should you be careful in countries that have mosquitoes?
4. How do viruses cause disease?
5. Give two examples of diseases caused by fungi.
6. What are plasmids?
7. What is a vector? Give an example.
8. Name three ways in which pathogens can enter the body.
9. If you had measles would you have been infected by a virus or a bacterium?
10. Name two diseases caused by bacteria.

CAUSES OF DISEASE — Biology

Defence against disease

The human body has many methods of *preventing pathogens* from entering the body.

If pathogens do get into the body then the *immune system* goes into action.

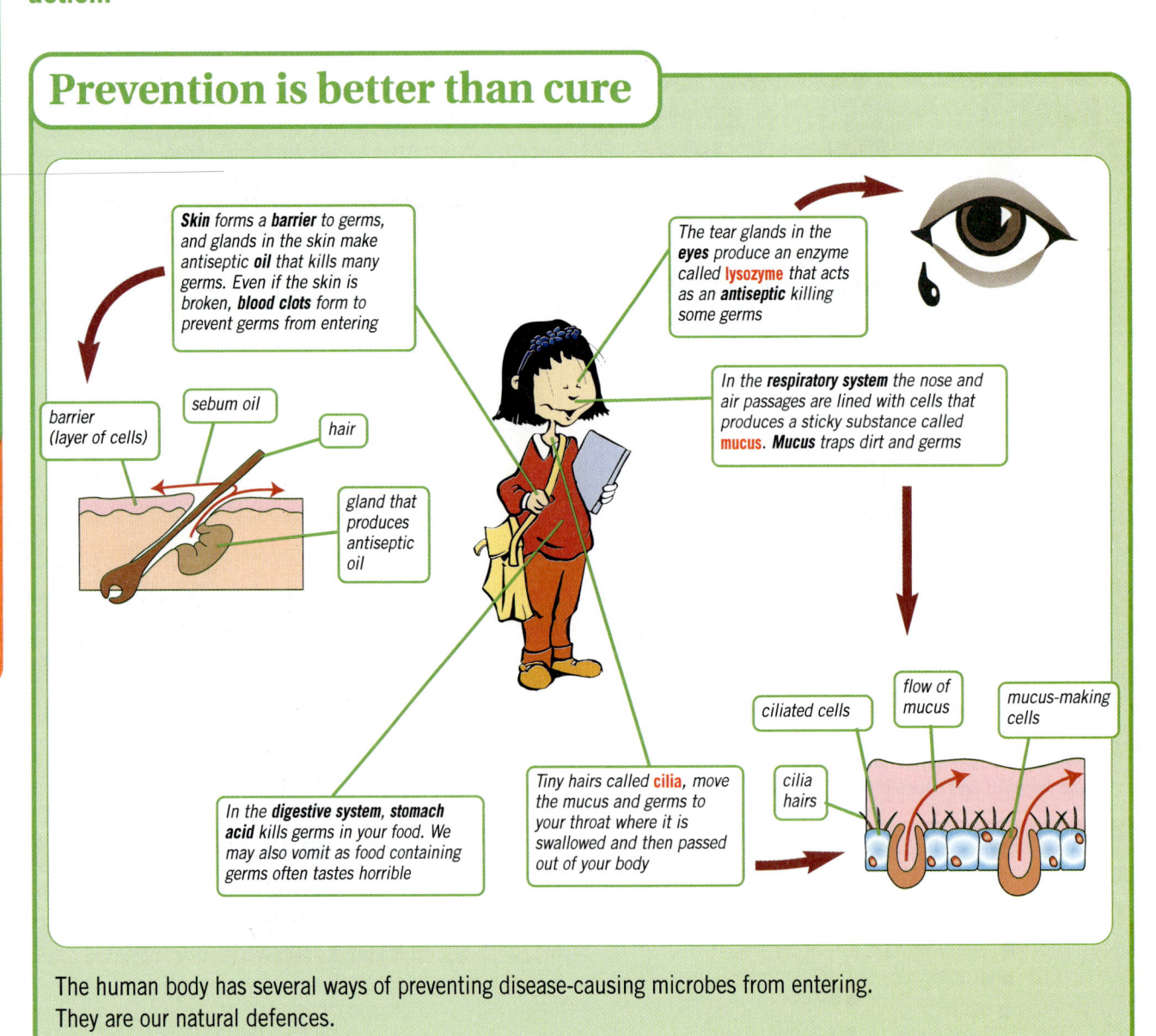

Prevention is better than cure

Skin forms a **barrier** to germs, and glands in the skin make antiseptic **oil** that kills many germs. Even if the skin is broken, **blood clots** form to prevent germs from entering

- barrier (layer of cells)
- sebum oil
- hair
- gland that produces antiseptic oil

The tear glands in the **eyes** produce an enzyme called **lysozyme** that acts as an **antiseptic** killing some germs

In the **respiratory system** the nose and air passages are lined with cells that produces a sticky substance called **mucus**. Mucus traps dirt and germs

- ciliated cells
- flow of mucus
- mucus-making cells
- cilia hairs

Tiny hairs called **cilia**, move the mucus and germs to your throat where it is swallowed and then passed out of your body

In the **digestive system**, **stomach acid** kills germs in your food. We may also vomit as food containing germs often tastes horrible

The human body has several ways of preventing disease-causing microbes from entering. They are our natural defences.

Preventing the spread of germs

We can **sterilise** equipment used in food preparation or in operating theatres by heating things to a temperature of 120°C.

We can use **disinfectants** on work surfaces and areas where germs thrive, such as toilets.

Antiseptics can kill germs on living tissue if we cut ourselves.

General good hygiene is important in preventing the spread of disease. Examples include washing hands after going to the toilet, cooking food thoroughly and keeping food in the fridge or freezer. These methods prevent bacteria from multiplying and causing disease.

The immune system response

If pathogens get into the body then the **white blood cells** travelling around in the blood spring into action.

White blood cells can make chemicals called **antitoxins** that destroy the toxins produced by bacteria.

White blood cells called **phagocytes** engulf the odd bacteria or viruses before they have a chance to do any harm.

However, if they are in large numbers then the other type of white blood cell called **lymphocytes** is involved.

All germs have chemicals on their surface called **antigens** and lymphocytes recognise these antigens as being foreign.

Lymphocytes produce chemicals called antibodies that attach to these antigens and clump them together.

Phagocytes can then engulf and destroy the bacteria and viruses.

Antibodies are specific to antigens.

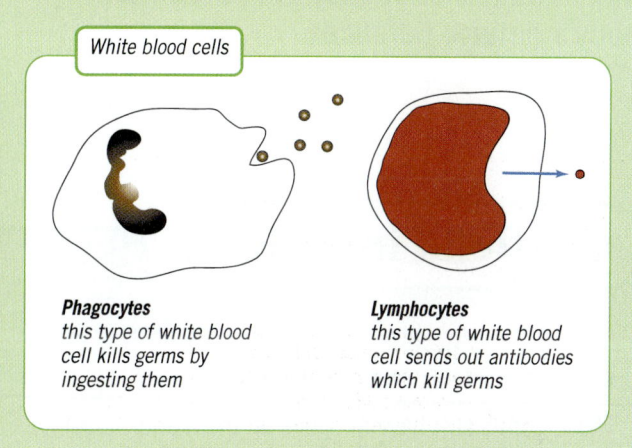

White blood cells

Phagocytes
this type of white blood cell kills germs by ingesting them

Lymphocytes
this type of white blood cell sends out antibodies which kill germs

Natural immunity

Making antibodies takes time, which is why you feel ill at first, and then get better as the disease is destroyed by the white blood cells.

Once a particular antibody is made it stays in your body. If the same disease enters your body again, the antibodies are much quicker at destroying it and you feel no symptoms. **You are now immune to that disease**.

Ways of preventing infection comes up often in the exam so make sure you are clear how the body prevents infection from getting in and causing disease.

KEY TERMS

Make sure you understand these terms before moving on!
- pathogens
- lysozyme
- mucus
- cilia
- antiseptics
- immune system response
- phagocytes
- lymphocytes
- natural immunity

QUICK TEST

1. How does the skin protect against disease?
2. What is the job of mucus?
3. Name four ways of preventing the spread of germs.
4. Name the two types of white blood cell that are involved in the immune response.
5. How do phagocytes kill germs?
6. What chemicals do white blood cells produce?
7. What do antitoxins do?
8. What is the role of antibodies?
9. Why do you tend to get some diseases only once, like measles?
10. How does the body recognise foreign bacteria and viruses?

DEFENCE AGAINST DISEASE

Biology

17

Treatment of disease

There are various ways of treating disease and infection once they get passed the body's natural defences.

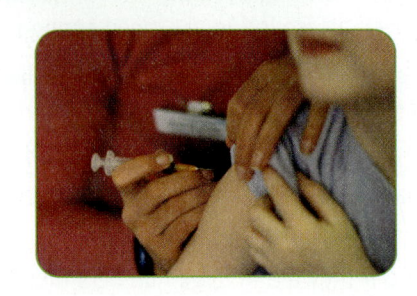

Artificial immunity

Artificial immunity involves the use of **vaccines**.

A **vaccine** contains dead or harmless germs.

These germs still have antigens on them and the white blood cells respond to them as if they were alive by multiplying and producing antibodies.

A vaccine is an advanced warning so that if the person is infected by the germ the white blood cells can **respond immediately** and kill them.

Vaccinations are an example of **passive immunity** as you produce your own antibodies and are fighting the disease yourself. An injection of ready made antibodies is called **active immunity**.

Vaccines help prevent the spread of disease and epidemics but it is a person's choice to decide on vaccinations for themselves or their children.

Some people argue that it is improved sanitation and hygiene that has led to the decrease of some diseases, and not vaccinations.

The vaccine to treat MMR (measles, mumps and rubella) is a viral vaccine and is causing controversy because of the side effects of using the triple vaccine instead of three separate ones. There is also the problem of possible side effects of all vaccines.

New vaccines against flu are needed regularly as the virus changes regularly. HIV vaccines are difficult as HIV has a high mutation rate and damages the immune system.

Antibiotics

Sometimes bacteria get through the body's defences and reproduce successfully.

In this case, outside help is needed to kill the germs in the form of **antibiotics**.

Antibiotics kill the germs without harming the body cells.

Penicillin was the first form of antibiotic. It is made from a mould called *Penicillium notatum*.

Antibiotics cannot treat infections caused by viruses. The body has to fight these on its own.

Mutations

Antibiotics can kill most bacteria but, as we continue to use them, bacteria are becoming **resistant** to them.

New antibiotics are constantly needed to fight the battle against bacteria.

There is a need for careful use of antibiotics as overuse has led to the highly resistant MRSA developing. MRSA is a 'superbug' that thrives in unhygienic conditions and is highly contagious. Places such as hospitals need scrupulous hygiene to try and prevent it developing and spreading

Bird flu, or Avian flu, is causing concern and there are worries that it may become a pandemic and affect many areas of the world. The main concern is that if the bird flu virus infects humans who have the human flu virus, it may mutate. This new strain may then be easily transmitted from human to human.

Drug testing

New drugs and medical treatments have to be extensively tested and trialled before being used. They are tested in the laboratory before being tested on human volunteers.

They are first tested on healthy volunteers to test for safety and then on people with the illness to test for effectiveness. The tests are normally 'blind' or 'double blind' where neither the patients nor the doctors know which are being treated. The patients are still receiving their normal treatment for their disease.

Placebos (a control group who receive a dummy drug that will not have any affect) are not often used as patients must still receive treatment.

Sometimes the tests fail, as in the case of **thalidomide**, a drug developed as a sleeping pill. It was found to be effective at treating morning sickness, however, it had not been tested for this use. This drug caused severe limb abnormalities in babies born to mothers taking the drug and was then banned. It is now more recently being used to treat leprosy and some forms of cancer.

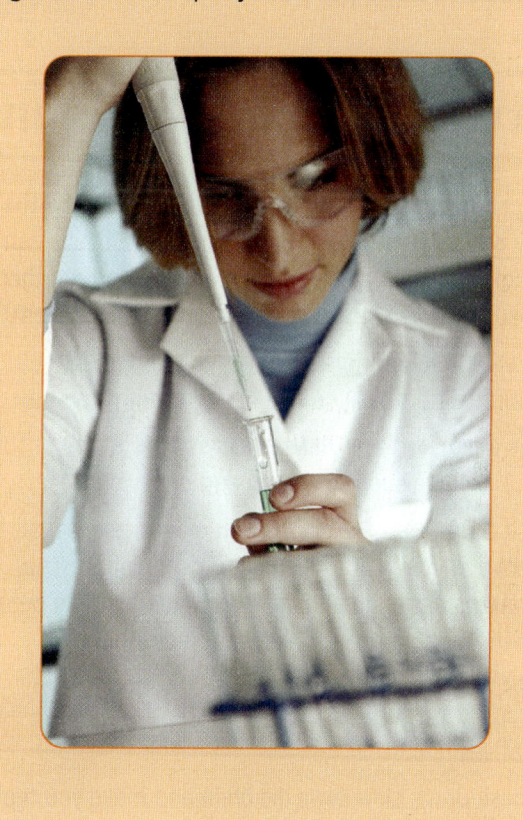

Scientific concept

In 1847, Dr. Semmelweiss suggested that hand washing prevented infection. He discovered this while delivering babies. There seemed to be a spread of childhood fever that was significantly reduced when hands were washed between patients. He suggested the modern day idea of disinfecting hands and instruments.

Make sure you know the difference between natural immunity and artificial immunity.

KEY TERMS

Make sure you understand these terms before moving on!
- artificial immunity
- vaccine
- passive immunity
- active immunity
- antibiotics
- penicillin
- drug testing

QUICK TEST

1. What does MMR stand for?
2. What is the main objection to the MMR vaccine?
3. What was the first form of antibiotic called?
4. How do bacteria and viruses become resistant to antibiotics?
5. Why do you think antibiotics are not used to treat viruses? (Hint: look back at the Causes of disease)
6. What do vaccines contain?
7. What does the term 'double blind' mean?
8. What is a placebo?
9. Why was thalidomide banned?
10. Are vaccinations an example of passive or active immunity?

TREATMENT OF DISEASE — Biology

Drugs

Smoking and solvents damage health, without a doubt.

Alcohol and drugs are also dangerous if misused for either recreational or pharmaceutical purposes.

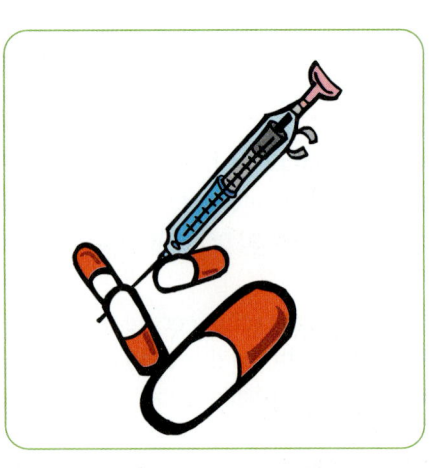

Drugs - why are they dangerous?

Drugs are powerful chemicals; they alter the way the body works, often without you realising it. Drugs can become **addictive**; people become dependent on them and suffer from withdrawal symptoms without them.

There are useful drugs such as penicillin and antibiotics but these can be dangerous if misused.

Drugs affect the brain and nervous system, which in turn affect aspects such as driving and behaviour.

Some drugs are taken for recreation and are illegal, but others are legal, such as alcohol and nicotine. The overall impact on health can be greater as more people take these drugs than the illegal drugs.

Drugs fall into four main groups:

Sedatives

- These drugs **slow down the brain** and make you feel sleepy, e.g. tranquillisers and sleeping pills.
- Barbiturates, which are powerful sedatives, are used as anaesthetics in hospitals.
- These drugs seriously alter reaction times and give you poor judgement of speed and distances.

Painkillers

- These drugs **suppress the pain sensors in the brain**, e.g. aspirin, heroin and morphine.
- Morphine is given to people in cases of extreme pain.
- Heroin can be injected which can increase the risk of contracting HIV; it is also highly addictive.

Hallucinogens

- These drugs **make you see or hear things that don't exist (have hallucinations)**, e.g. ecstasy, LSD and cannabis.
- The hallucinations can lead to fatal accidents.

Stimulants

- These drugs **speed up the brain and nervous system** and make you more alert and awake, e.g. amphetamines, cocaine and the less harmful caffeine in tea and coffee.
- Dependence on these drugs is high, and withdrawing from them causes serious depression.

Drugs and the law

Drugs are classified in law as class A, class B and class C.

- Class A drugs, such as heroin, carry the most severe penalties if you are caught in possession. Supplying these drugs can lead to life imprisonment.
- Class B drugs, such as amphetamines, still carry severe penalties with up to 14 years imprisonment.
- Recently, cannabis has become a class C drug carrying less harsh penalties if caught in possession. However, if it is in possession with intent to supply, the penalty is up to 14 years imprisonment.

The cannabis debate still continues about whether it is harmful, addictive or whether it leads on to harder drugs such as heroin. At present, health professionals cannot agree. However, it is said to be psychologically addictive and if taken with nicotine, the nicotine makes it physically addictive. Some people argue that it is a useful pain relief drug for the terminally ill but the medical opinion fluctuates.

Solvents

Solvents include everyday products like glue and aerosols.

Solvent fumes are inhaled and are absorbed by the lungs.

They soon reach the brain and **slow down breathing and heart rates**.

They also damage the **kidneys and liver**.

Repeated inhalation can cause loss of control and unconsciousness.

Many first time inhalers die from heart failure or suffocation if using aerosols.

Many of the symptoms are likened to being drunk, vomiting may occur and the person may not be in control.

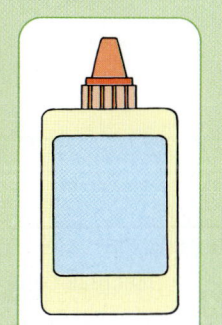

Solvent fumes, like glue and aerosols, reach the brain

Alcohol

Alcohol is a **depressant** and reduces the activity of the brain and nervous system.

It is absorbed through the gut and taken to the brain in the blood.

Alcohol damages neurones in the brain and causes irreversible brain damage.

The liver breaks down alcohol at the rate of one unit an hour but an excess of alcohol has a very **damaging effect on the liver, called cirrhosis**.

Each of these drinks contains one unit of alcohol
- ½ pint cider (0.3 litre)
- 1 glass of sherry
- 1 glass of wine
- ½ pint beer (0.3 litre)
- 1 single whisky

Increasing amounts of alcohol causes people to lose control and slur their words. In this state accidents are more likely to happen.

Smoking

Tobacco, without a doubt, causes health problems.

It contains many harmful chemicals: **nicotine** is an addictive substance and a mild stimulant, **tar** is known to contain carcinogens that contribute to cancer and **carbon monoxide** that prevents the red blood cells from carrying oxygen.

If pregnant women smoke then carbon monoxide deprives the foetus of oxygen and can lead to a low birth mass.

Some diseases caused by smoking include **emphysema, bronchitis, heart and blood vessel problems, and lung cancer**.

The link between smoking and lung cancer is now becoming widely accepted. Tobacco contains carcinogens, chemicals that cause cancer. According to Cancer Research UK it causes 9 out of 10 lung cancers.

Ways to stop smoking include using nicotine replacement products such as patches or chewing gum, using coping skills to deal with triggers that make you smoke, the use of rewards, having a support system, hypnotherapy, gradual reduction in nicotine or just giving up completely ('cold turkey').

Concentrate on the health problems for the exam, but the social aspects are still important.

KEY TERMS

Make sure you understand these terms before moving on!
- addictive
- depressant
- cirrhosis
- carbon monoxide
- lung cancer

QUICK TEST

1. Which parts of the body are affected by alcohol?
2. What drug class does cannabis fall into?
3. Name three chemicals contained in tobacco.
4. What diseases does smoking cause?
5. What is the name of the disease of the liver?

DRUGS — Biology

Genetic engineering

Genetic engineering is the process in which genes from one organism are removed and inserted into the cells of another.

It has many exciting possibilities but it is not without its problems.

Scientists can now genetically modify plants and animals using the process of genetic engineering.

Manipulating genes

Our genes code for a particular protein that enables all our normal life processes to function.

Many diseases are caused when the body cannot make a particular protein.

Genetic engineering has been used to treat people with diabetes by the production of the protein, **insulin**.

The gene that codes for insulin can be found in the human pancreas cells.

Other human proteins made in this way include a human growth hormone that is used to treat children who do not grow properly.

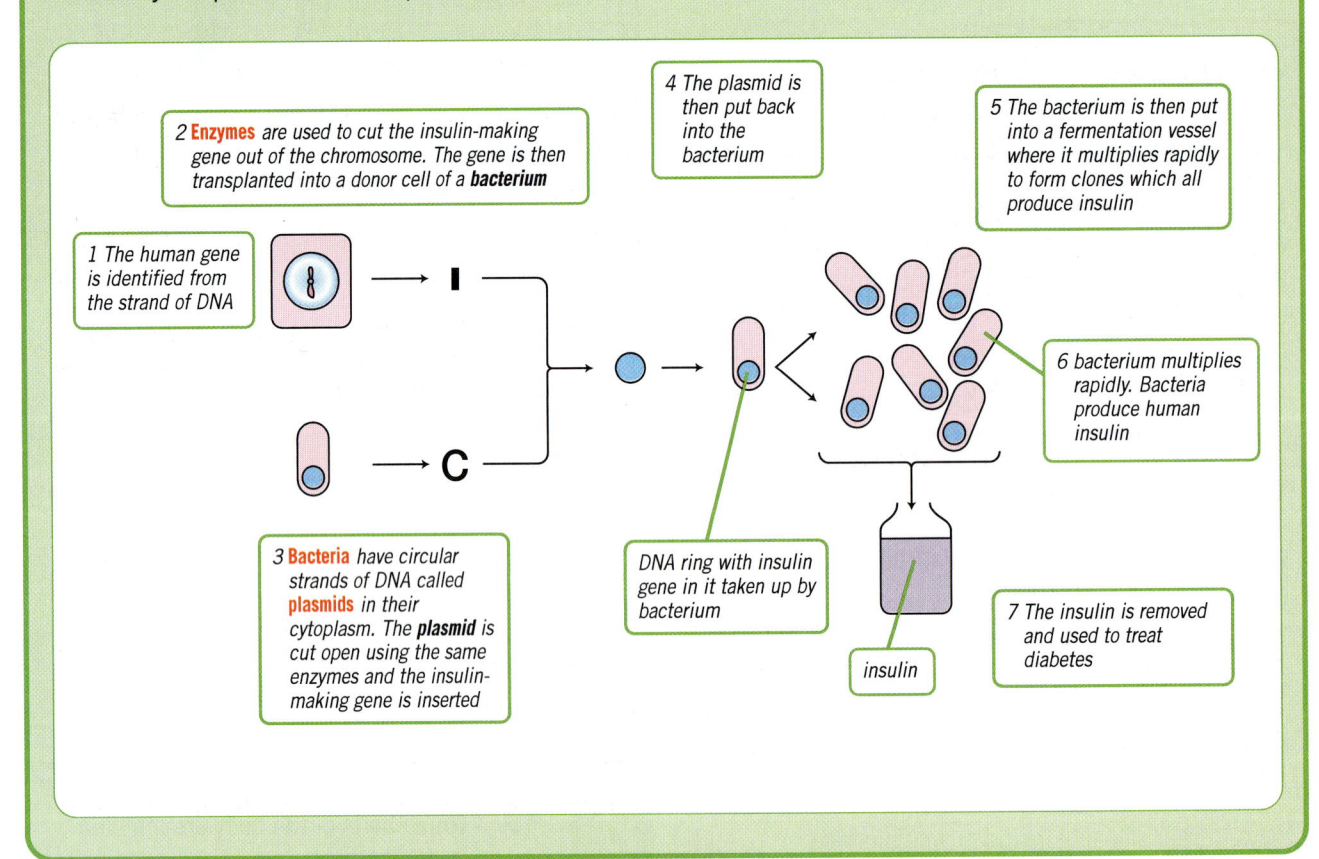

1 The human gene is identified from the strand of DNA

2 **Enzymes** are used to cut the insulin-making gene out of the chromosome. The gene is then transplanted into a donor cell of a **bacterium**

3 **Bacteria** have circular strands of DNA called **plasmids** in their cytoplasm. The **plasmid** is cut open using the same enzymes and the insulin-making gene is inserted

4 The plasmid is then put back into the bacterium

DNA ring with insulin gene in it taken up by bacterium

5 The bacterium is then put into a fermentation vessel where it multiplies rapidly to form clones which all produce insulin

6 bacterium multiplies rapidly. Bacteria produce human insulin

7 The insulin is removed and used to treat diabetes

insulin

GM crops

Presently there are no genetically modified crops grown in the UK and there are no plans to grow them until 2008. However, they have been grown for research and development purposes.

Countries that do grow **GM crops** include the USA, Argentina, Canada and China. What they grow, and and in what quantities, varies form country to country but the crops include corn, cotton and soya bean.

The benefits of genetic engineering

Genetic engineering benefits industry, medicine and agriculture in many ways.

- We have developed plants that are resistant to pests and diseases and plants that can grow in less desirable conditions.
- Wheat and other crops have been developed that can take nitrogen directly from the air and produce proteins without the need of costly fertilisers.
- Tomatoes and other sorts of fruit are now able to stay fresh for longer.
- Animals are engineered to produce chemicals in their milk such as drugs and human antibodies.

Tomatoes can be genetically engineered to stay fresh for longer by inserting a gene from fish into their cells. Would you eat one?

The list seems endless and there is no doubt as to the benefits of genetic engineering now and in the future, but there are also risks and moral issues that are associated with this relatively modern technology.

Risks of genetic engineering

Manipulating bacteria for use in producing proteins might result in previously harmless bacteria mutating into a disease-causing bacteria.

- There is concern about the damage to human health, with GM crops causing allergies and the notion of eating 'foreign' DNA. Also will the nutritional quality still be there?
- There is also concern about the damage to the environment; crops may cross pollinate with weeds and transfer the gene that gives resistance to herbicides and pesticides.

Gene therapy is, potentially, a way forward in curing fatal diseases, but it poses risks as inserting genes into human cells may make them cancerous.

There is a possibility that a human egg can be taken out of the womb and the harmful genes removed before it is inserted back in the womb to continue its growth into a human.

Genetic engineering is seen by many as manipulating the stuff of life: is it **morally or ethically wrong** to interfere with nature?

There is still a lot of unease about the methods used as nobody can be completely sure what the results will be.

> *You may be asked to provide arguments for and against the use of genetic engineering so be prepared to discuss the benefits and risks involved.*

KEY TERMS

Make sure you understand these terms before moving on!
- insulin
- enzymes
- bacteria
- plasmids
- GM crops
- ethically

QUICK TEST

1. What is the circular DNA of a bacterium called?
2. What does the GM stand for in GM crops?
3. How are human genes 'cut out'?
4. How could weeds benefit from GM crops?
5. Name a disease that has the potential to be treated using genetic engineering.
6. What are the benefits of developing crops that are resistant to frost?
7. Where is the insulin gene found in humans?
8. Give an example of the use of bacteria to treat a disease.
9. What are the risks associated with using bacteria to produce human proteins?
10. What is gene therapy?

GENETIC ENGINEERING | Biology

Genes

- We inherit genes from our parents.
- Genes are the chemical instructions that control all our characteristics.

The relationship between genes, chromosomes and DNA

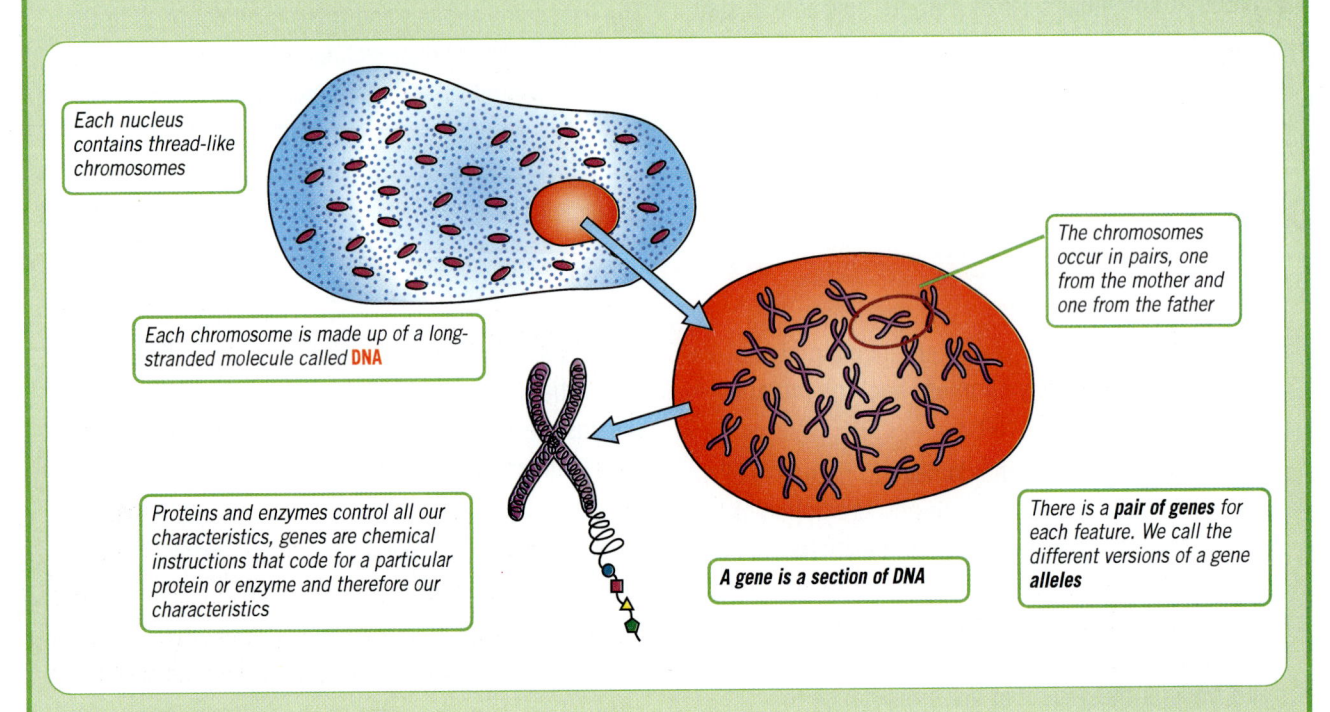

Each nucleus contains thread-like chromosomes

Each chromosome is made up of a long-stranded molecule called **DNA**

Proteins and enzymes control all our characteristics, genes are chemical instructions that code for a particular protein or enzyme and therefore our characteristics

The chromosomes occur in pairs, one from the mother and one from the father

A gene is a section of DNA

There is a **pair of genes** for each feature. We call the different versions of a gene **alleles**

Inside nearly all cells is a **nucleus**.

The nucleus **contains instructions** that control all your characteristics.

The instructions are carried on **chromosomes**.

Genes on the chromosome control each particular **characteristic**.

Different genes control the development of different characteristics.

Inside human cells there are **46 chromosomes** or **23 pairs**. The cell is called a diploid cell.

Other animals have different numbers of chromosomes.

Inheritance

To inherit characteristics from parents' DNA some form of reproduction needs to take place. There are two forms:

- **Asexual reproduction** involves only one parent; the offspring have exact copies of the parental genes. There is no fusing (joining) of the parental **gametes** (sperm and eggs).
- Asexual reproduction produces clones, there is no variation.

- **Sexual reproduction** involves fertilisation and two parents. The gametes' nuclei fuse and the genes are passed on to the offspring. The offspring are not genetically identical.
- Sexual reproduction leads to variation not only between different species of plants and animals but also between individuals of the same species.
- The differences are partly due to the **inheritance** of genes from the parents but also to the **environments** in which the offspring live and grow.

DNA molecule

- A coiled up DNA molecule makes up the 'arms' of a chromosome.
- A DNA molecule is joined together by chemical bases like rungs in a ladder.
- The two arms of the ladder are coiled together to form a **double helix**.
- There are four bases: adenine A, cytosine C, guanine G, and thymine T.
- A always pairs with T and G always pairs with C.

DNA has the ability to copy itself exactly so that any new cells made have exactly the same genetic information.

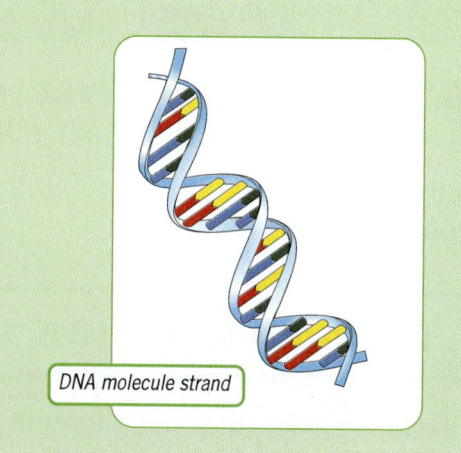

DNA molecule strand

GENES Biology

Mutations

DNA is a very stable molecule, but occasionally things can go wrong in the copying process.

A mutation is a change in the chemical structure of a gene or chromosome, which alters the way an organism develops.

The change may happen for no reason or there might be a definite cause.

- Mutations occur naturally in the environment, for example new strains of the flu virus are always appearing.
- Mutations that occur to body cells are not inherited; they are only harmful to the person whose body cells are altered.
- Mutations that occur in reproductive cells are inherited; the child will develop abnormally or die at an early age.

Some mutations that are inherited are beneficial and form the basis of evolution.

- Organisms that become adapted to the environment are more able to survive and pass on their genes.
- The peppered moth's allele for dark colouring gave it an advantage over the white moth when its environment became more polluted (see Evidence for evolution spread on page 30).

There are lots of key words on this page that are new, learn their definitions.

KEY TERMS

Make sure you understand these terms before moving on!
- nucleus
- chromosomes
- genes
- DNA
- asexual reproduction
- sexual reproduction
- gametes

QUICK TEST

1. What are the thread-like features contained in the nucleus called?
2. What actually controls all our characteristics?
3. What are genes?
4. Where are genes found?
5. In what circumstances are mutations inherited?
6. How many chromosomes does a human body cell have and where are they found?
7. How many genes are there for each feature in question 6?
8. What are the human gametes?
9. Which type of reproduction produces clones?
10. Which type of reproduction formed you? What else has an effect on how you look and behave?

Selective breeding

Selective breeding is where we breed in the features that we want in a plant or animal and breed out features that we don't want.

Humans do the selecting rather than nature so we call it *artificial selection*.

Artificial selection

People are always trying to breed animals and plants with special characteristics, e.g. a fast racehorse or a cow that produces lots of milk.

Breeding has to be carried out within the same species, different species can't breed together. The procedures involved in artificial selection are:

- Select the individuals with the best characteristics.
- Breed them together using sexual reproduction.
- Hopefully some of the offspring will have inherited some of the desirable features; the best offspring are selected and are bred together.
- This is repeated over generations until the offspring have all the desired characteristics.

Selective breeding in animals

The farm pig has been selectively bred over the years from a wild pig.

wild pig

modern farm pig

The features that have been bred in are:

- less hair
- a quieter temperament
- more fat.

Can you think why?

- Cows have been selectively bred to produce a greater quantity of milk.

- Beef cattle have been bred to produce better meat.

The problem with only breeding from the best cows and bulls is that the cows can only give birth once a year, so new techniques have been developed.

Dolly the sheep

Dolly the sheep was the first mammal cloned in 1996; she died prematurely in 2003. Her early death fuelled the debate about long term health problems of clones. The procedure to create her is as follows:

- The nucleus was removed from an egg cell.
- The egg cell nucleus was replaced with the nucleus of an udder cell.
- This cell was then implanted into another sheep.
- The cell then grew into a clone of the sheep from which the udder cell came.

Embryo transfer

The process for **embryo transfer** is as follows:

- The sperm is taken from the best bull.
- The best cow is given hormones to produce lots of eggs.
- The eggs are removed from the cow and are fertilised in a petri dish.
- The embryos are allowed to develop but are then split apart to form clones before they become specialised.
- The embryos are then implanted into other cows, called surrogates, where they grow into the desired offspring.

Advantages are: the sperm and the eggs can be frozen to be used at a later date and a large number of offspring can be produced from one bull and one cow.

Selective breeding in plants

Selectively bred individuals may not always produce the desired characteristics because sexual reproduction always produces variation.

With plants this can be overcome by producing clones.

Clones are genetically identical individuals.

To produce clones, asexual reproduction is needed.

Many plants reproduce asexually on their own, such as strawberry plants that produce runners.

Tissue culture

Gardeners can produce new identical plants by taking **cuttings** from the original parent plant.

The plants are dipped in rooting powder containing hormones and are kept in a damp atmosphere to grow into new plants. The new plants would be clones.

Tissue culture is a technique used by commercial plant breeders.

They take just a few plant cells and grow a new plant from them, using a special growth medium containing hormones.

The advantages are that new plants can be grown quickly and cheaply all year round with special properties such as resistance to diseases.

Plants also produce sexually, attracting insects for pollination.

The resulting plants show variation.

This is very important because if they only produced clones and a new disease developed, it would kill the one clone and therefore the entire species as they would be all the same.

Problems with selective breeding

The problem is a reduction in the number of alleles in a population.

- If animals or plants are continually bred from the same best animals or plants then the animals and plants will all be very similar.
- If there is a change in the environment, then the new animals and plants may not be able to cope with it.
- There may be no alleles left to selectively breed new varieties of plants and animals, so it is important to keep wild varieties alive.

Make sure you can list the advantages of the methods of selective breeding and also the disadvantages.

Scientific concept

The implications of cloning Dolly are that scientists are looking at ways of using genetically engineered animals to grow replacement organs for humans. This poses many ethical concerns, not least the problems of tissue rejection. What do you think?

QUICK TEST

1. What is selective breeding?
2. What is the difference between artificial selection and natural selection?
3. What are clones?
4. Name a technique used in the selective breeding of animals.
5. Name two methods of selective breeding in plants.
6. What is the main disadvantage of selective breeding?
7. When a gardener takes cuttings is he using sexual reproduction or asexual reproduction to grow new plants?
8. Give a reason why embryo transfer are used to produce cows and bulls.

KEY TERMS

Make sure you understand these terms before moving on!
- selective breeding
- artificial selection
- embryo transfer
- clones
- cuttings
- tissue culture

Evolution

Evolution is all about change and improvement from simple life forms.

The *theory of evolution* states that all living things that exist today, or once existed, evolved from simple life forms three billion years ago.

Natural selection is the process that causes evolution.

The theory of evolution

Natural selection, as demonstrated in the wild

- there is a struggle for existence
- organisms with useful characteristics are more likely to survive and pass them on to the next generation
- organisms produce a large number of offspring
- in any species there is a variation between individuals

Religious theories are based on the need for a 'creator' for all life to exist on earth, but there are other theories.

Charles Darwin, a British naturalist, first put forward his theory about 140 years ago. Charles visited the Galapagos Islands, off the coast of South America, and made a number of observations that led to his theory of evolution.

They were:

- Organisms produce more offspring than could possibly survive.
- Population numbers remain fairly constant despite this.
- All organisms in a species show **variation**.
- Some of these variations are inherited.

He also concluded from these observations that since there were more offspring produced than could survive; there must be a struggle for existence.

This led to the strongest and fittest offspring surviving and passing on their genes to their offspring. This is sometimes called the **Survival of the Fittest** or **Natural Selection**.

The combined effects of natural selection, selective breeding, genetic engineering and mutations may lead to a new **species** forming.

Other theories

- In the 17th century, Archbishop James Usher said that God created all life forms from the simple to the complex. He thought that life began on Monday October 3rd 4004 BC.
- In the 18th century, Conte De Buffon, a French zoologist, thought that living things changed over time due to the environment or chance. He also thought that humans and apes were related.
- Erasmus Darwin (Charles' father) believed in evolution but did not know what caused it.
- Later, reasons for organisms evolving started to focus on natural disasters and changes to the Earth. It was thought that some organisms were killed off by these changes and new life forms developed. Fossil evidence also became more important. This was getting closer to Charles Darwin's theory of natural selection.

Natural selection

Darwin stated that the process of natural selection was the basis for evolution.

- A species is defined as a group of living things that are able to breed together and produce fertile offspring.
- Within a species there is variation between individuals.
- Changes in the environment may affect some individuals and not others.
- **Only those who can adapt to suit their new environment survive to breed and pass on their advantageous genes.**

Other factors that tend to prevent all offspring surviving are:

- **competition for food**
- **predators**
- **disease.**

Eventually it seems that nature has decided which individuals should survive and breed. There is a **survival of the fittest**.

Scientific concept

Darwin's theory became widely accepted eventually but a man called **Lamarck** suggested that animals evolved features according to how much they used them, for example giraffes grew longer necks because they needed to reach food.

KEY TERMS

Make sure you understand these terms before moving on!

- evolution
- natural selection
- Charles Darwin
- species
- Lamarck

QUICK TEST

1. When did life forms first exist?
2. Whose theory of evolution was gradually accepted?
3. What prevents all the organisms in a species surviving?
4. Which individuals would survive a change in the environment?
5. What process causes evolution?
6. Where in the world did Darwin make observations that led to his theory?
7. Define the word species.
8. What was Darwin's observation when he looked at the individuals in a species?
9. Why was there a struggle for existence within a population?
10. Does evolution happen gradually or does it occur suddenly?

Evidence for evolution

Charles Darwin's theory of evolution is now widely accepted.

Fossils provide the evidence for evolution.

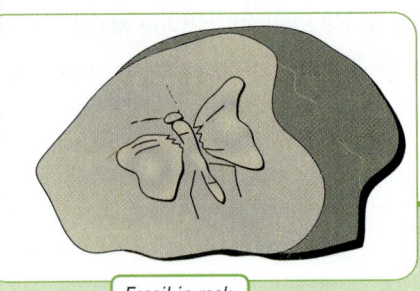

Fossils

Fossils are the remains of dead organisms that lived millions of years ago. They are found in rocks.

Most dead organisms decay and disintegrate, but the following are ways that fossils can be formed:

- The hard parts of animals that don't decay form into a rock.
- Minerals which preserve their shape gradually replace the softer parts of animals that decay very slowly.
- In areas where one or more of the conditions needed for decay are absent, for example areas where there is **no oxygen, moisture or warmth**.

Fossils provide **evidence** for evolution. They are preserved in rock with generally the younger fossils being found near the surface.

The evolution of the horse is clearly shown by fossils.

- Look at the changes in their size and feet caused by the changes in the environment over the years.
- **Natural selection** has operated to produce the modern horse.

Fossil in rock

The modern horse: an example of natural selection

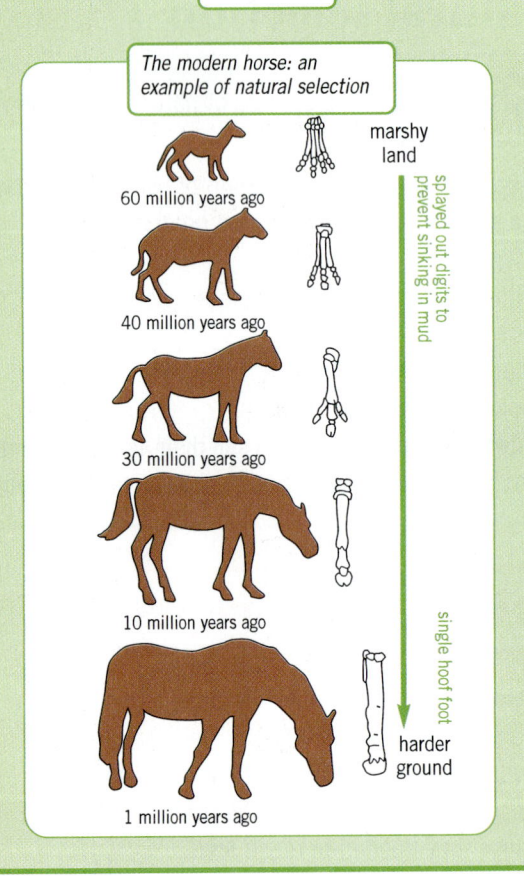

60 million years ago
40 million years ago
30 million years ago
10 million years ago
1 million years ago

marshy land — splayed out digits to prevent sinking in mud

single hoof foot — harder ground

Natural selection in action

An example of the environment causing changes in a species is the **peppered moth**.

They live in woodlands on lichen-covered trees.

There are two types of peppered moth, a light, speckled form and a dark form.

The dark-coloured moth was caused by a mutation and was usually eaten by predators.

In the 1850s the dark type of moth was rare, but pollution from factories started to blacken tree trunks.

The dark moth was then at an advantage because it was camouflaged.

Pollution played a key role in the 'survival of the fittest' for these peppered moths

dark-coloured moth against a soot-covered tree

the pale moth is at a disadvantage in polluted areas

In 1895 most of the population of moths was dark.

In cleaner areas the light moth had an advantage against predators so it survived to breed.

Mutations

Mutations that occur in genes are usually harmful, but in the case of the peppered moth it turned out to be useful when the environment changed.

Over a long period of time, gradual changes (mutations) may result in totally new species being formed.

This brings us back to the theory of evolution; that all species evolved from a common ancestor that existed billions of years ago.

Those species that were unable to adapt to their surroundings became extinct.

Extinction

Species that are unable to adapt to their surroundings become extinct.

Examples include the mammoth, the dodo and the sabre-toothed tiger.

Extinction can also be caused by changes in the environment, new predators, new diseases, new competition, or human activity, e.g. hunting, pollution or habitat destruction.

The peppered moth and the evolution of the horse are popular examples to demonstrate evolution by natural selection.

mammoth

Extinct animals

sabre-toothed tiger

dodo

KEY TERMS

Make sure you understand these terms before moving on!
- fossils
- evidence
- natural selection
- peppered moth
- mutations
- extinction

QUICK TEST

1. Why did the feet of the modern horse change?
2. Which type of peppered moth would survive in industrial regions and why?
3. What conditions need to be **absent** for fossils to be formed?
4. What is the prime reason why organisms become extinct?
5. What are fossils?
6. Is it possible for fossils to be formed in the Arctic?
7. What caused the light peppered moth to change colour?
8. How could humans cause a species to become extinct?
9. Where are young fossils found in relation to older fossils?
10. What process has led to produce the modern day horse?

EVIDENCE FOR EVOLUTION — Biology

Adaptation and competition

A *habitat* is where an organism lives; it has the conditions needed for it to survive.

A *community* consists of living things in the *habitat*.

Each *community* is made up of different *populations of animals and plants*.

Each *population* is adapted to live in that particular *habitat*.

Sizes of populations

Population numbers cannot keep growing out of control; factors that keep the population from becoming too large are called limiting factors. The factors that affect the size of a population are:

- Amount of food and water available
- Predators or grazing - who may eat the animal or plant
- Disease
- Climate, temperature, floods, droughts and storms
- Competition for space, mates, light, food and water

- Human activity such as pollution or destruction of habitats.

Organisms will only live and reproduce where conditions are suitable; the amount of light, temperature and availability of food and water will affect the organism and are essential for their survival.

These factors vary in time of day and year; this helps explain why organisms vary from place to place, and are restricted to certain habitats. Organisms have adapted to live in certain areas.

Adaptation

You never see a polar bear in the desert or a camel at the North Pole. This is because they are not adapted to live there.

They have adapted to live where they do; they have **special features** that help them survive.

The polar bear: adapted to deal with arctic conditions

A polar bear lives in cold arctic regions of the world; it has many features that enable it to survive:

- It has a **thick coat** to keep in body heat as well as a **layer of blubber** for insulation.
- Its coat is **white** so that it can blend into its surroundings.
- Its **fur is greasy** so doesn't hold water after swimming. This prevents cooling by evaporation.
- A polar bear has **big feet** to spread its weight on snow and ice; it also has big **sharp claws** to catch fish.
- It is **good swimmer** and **runner** to catch prey.

- The shape of a polar bear is **compact** even though it is large. This keeps the surface area to a minimum to reduce loss of body heat.

A camel has features that enable it to survive in the hot deserts of the world.

- The camel has an ability to **drink** a lot of water and **store** it.
- It loses very little water as it produces **little urine** and it can cope with big changes in temperature so there is **no need for sweating**.
- All fat is stored in the humps so there is **no insulation layer**.
- Its **sandy** colour provides **camouflage**.
- It has a **large surface area** to enable it to lose heat.

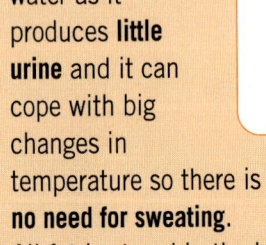

The camel: ideally suited to living in hot, dry deserts

In a community, the animal or plant best adapted to its surroundings will survive.

Competition

As populations grow, there may be overcrowding and limited resources to support the growing numbers.

Animals have to compete for **space, food and water** in their struggle to survive.

Only the strongest will survive, leading to the survival of the fittest.

Plants compete for **space, light, water and nutrients**.

The weed is a very successful competitor; look at the diagram to see how.

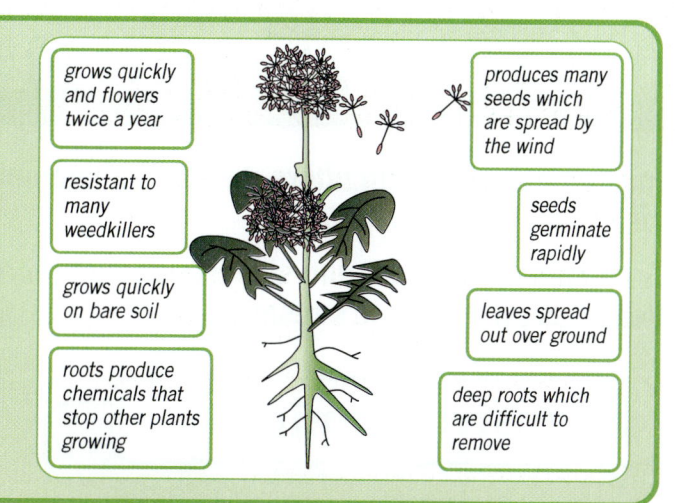

- grows quickly and flowers twice a year
- resistant to many weedkillers
- grows quickly on bare soil
- roots produce chemicals that stop other plants growing
- produces many seeds which are spread by the wind
- seeds germinate rapidly
- leaves spread out over ground
- deep roots which are difficult to remove

Predator/prey graphs

In a community the numbers of animals stays fairly constant; this is partly due to the amount of food limiting the size of the populations.

- **A predator** is an animal who hunts and kills another animal.
- **A prey** is the hunted animal.

Populations of predator and prey go in cycles.

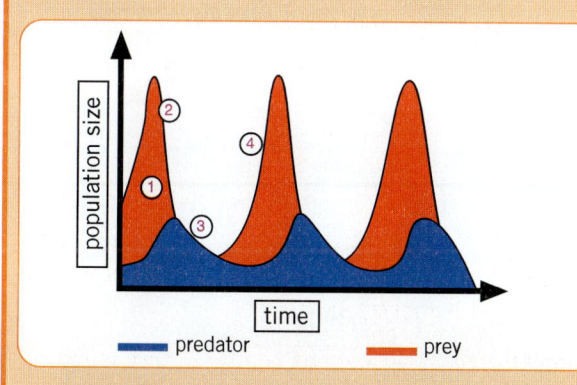

1. If the population of prey increases then there is more food for the predator so its numbers increase.
2. This causes the number of prey to decrease as they are eaten.
3. This causes the number of predators to decrease, as there is not enough food.
4. If the predator numbers fall then the prey numbers can increase again, as they are not being eaten, and so on.

- **Predators have adapted** to survive by being strong, agile and fast. They have good vision and a camouflaged body. They also hunt in packs, have a variety of prey and often hunt the young, sick and old.
- **Prey have also adapted**; the best adapted escape and breed. Adaptations of prey include: being able to run, swim and fly fast; they stay in large groups; they have a horrible taste; warning colours and camouflage.

The adaptations of a camel and a polar bear are popular examples for the exam, but be aware that there are other animals and plants that have adapted to live in environments.

Follow the **predator/prey graph** to see how the numbers of prey affect the numbers of predators and vice versa.

KEY TERMS

Make sure you understand these terms before moving on!

- population
- limiting factors
- competition
- adapted
- predator/prey graph

QUICK TEST

1. What is a habitat?
2. Define the word community.
3. What makes up a population?
4. What things do animals compete for?
5. What things do plants compete for?
6. If the number of prey increases what will happen to the number of predators?
7. Why do the numbers of prey and predators in a community stay fairly constant?
8. How does the polar bear's coat help it survive in the Arctic?

ADAPTATION AND COMPETITION — Biology

Environmental damage

Improvements in agriculture, health and medicine have meant a dramatic rise in the human population.

An increase in population size leads to an increase in pollution and demands on the world's resources.

Intensive farming

Farming has had to become more intensive to try and provide more food from a given area of land.

Intensive farming can produce more food but it has problems.

Many people regard intensive farming of animals as cruel.

In order to produce more food from the land, **fertilisers** and **pesticides** are needed.

Pesticides

Pesticides are used to kill insects that damage crops.

They also kill harmless insects, which can cause a shortage of food for insect-eating birds.

There is always the danger that pesticides can get washed into rivers and lakes and **end up in our food chains**.

This was the case in the 1960s when a pesticide called DDT got into the food chain and threatened populations of animals.

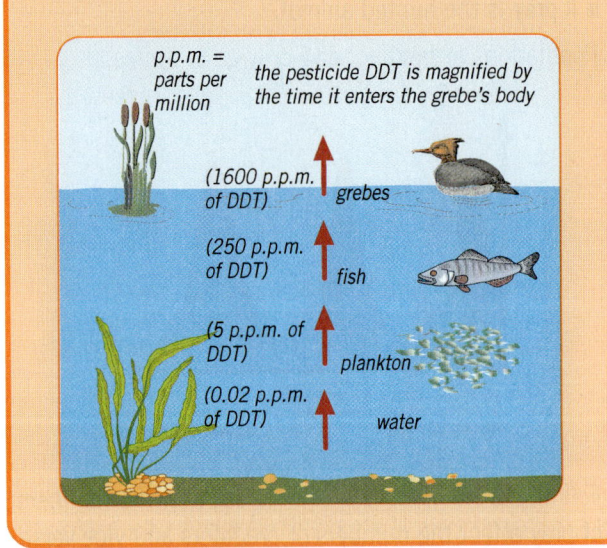

p.p.m. = parts per million — the pesticide DDT is magnified by the time it enters the grebe's body

- (1600 p.p.m. of DDT) grebes
- (250 p.p.m. of DDT) fish
- (5 p.p.m. of DDT) plankton
- (0.02 p.p.m. of DDT) water

Fertilisers

Plants need nutrients to grow which they take up from the soil.

With intensive farming methods, nutrients are quickly used up, so the farmer has to replace them with artificial fertilisers.

Fertilisers enable farmers to produce more crops in a smaller area of land and can reduce the need to destroy the countryside for extra space.

However, there are problems with the use of fertilisers particularly **eutrophication**.

Eutrophication

If too much fertiliser is added to the soil and it rains soon afterwards then the fertiliser finds its way into rivers and lakes. This causes the water plants to grow more quickly and cover the surface of the water.

More water plants means more competition for light and some plants die.

Microbes (bacteria and fungi) break down the dead plants and use up oxygen for respiration. This reduces the amount of oxygen available for animals and they die of suffocation.

Untreated sewage pumped into rivers and streams also causes **eutrophication**.

- lots of plant growth
- very little light below the surface
- dead plants sink to the bottom
- microbes break down dead plants and use up oxygen through respiration
- fish and other animals suffocate

Destruction of the land

An increase in industry has led to the need to take over the land which destroys wildlife and causes pollution.

we use land for building

dumping our rubbish

getting raw materials

farming to feed the world

What can be done?

The problems will get worse unless people can learn to limit their needs to prevent the destruction of our planet.

Intensive farming does produce quality food, more than enough to supply peoples' needs in Europe, but it also creates many problems.

A possible solution to some of the problems is **organic farming**.

- Organic farming produces less food per area of land and can be expensive, but it attempts to leave the countryside as it is and is kinder to animals.
- Organic farming uses **manure as a fertiliser**, **sets aside land** to allow wild plants and animals to flourish and uses **biological control of pests**.
- Biological control of pests is the use of other animals that eat pests; it is not so effective but produces no harmful effects.

Another method that could be used to reduce harm to the environment is the use of **greenhouses** to grow food efficiently and out of season.

We can also look at developing **alternative energy sources** such as solar power and wind energy. This will help conserve the world's rapidly diminishing fossil fuel supply.

Learn the arguments for and against intensive farming.

> *Don't forget about acid rain and the greenhouse effect as problems intensified by the growing human population.*

Deforestation

Already in the UK there are not many forests left. In under-developed countries they are **chopping down forests** (**deforestation**) to provide timber or space for agriculture for the growing numbers of people.

This causes several problems to the environment:

- Burning this timber increases the level of carbon dioxide in the air.
- Forests absorb carbon dioxide in the air, reducing the greenhouse effect and provide us with oxygen.
- Chopping down trees leads to soil erosion as the soil is exposed to rain and wind.
- Trees evaporate water into the air and without it there will be a decrease in rainfall.
- Destroying forests also destroys many different habitats of animals and plants.

KEY TERMS

Make sure you understand these terms before moving on!

- intensive farming
- fertilisers
- pesticides
- eutrophication
- deforestation
- organic farming

QUICK TEST

1. Why has the human population increased in the last few hundred years?
2. What problems can the use of pesticides cause?
3. How do fertilisers get into rivers and lakes?
4. What is the name of the process whereby fertilisers lead to the death of animals and plants in water?
5. Name four ways that humans reduce the amount of land.
6. What is deforestation?
7. How does deforestation contribute to the greenhouse effect?
8. What other problems does deforestation cause?
9. What could be used as an alternative to fertilisers?
10. Name ways in which we can reduce harmful effects on the environment.

ENVIRONMENTAL DAMAGE — Biology

Practice questions

Use the questions to test your progress. Check your answers on page 110.

1. What causes eutrophication?

2. What was Thalidomide first used for?

3. What does the technique embryo transfer involve?

4. Who was Dolly the sheep?

5. Is Kwashiorkor a developing world or a developed world problem?

6. Smoking during pregnancy is harmful to the foetus but in what particular way?

7. Where can the animal the dodo be found?

8. What is meant by the term 'active immunity'?

9. If you were to eat a diet rich in saturated fats what would the effects be?

10. What do the letters CNS stand for and what does it consist of?

11. Name the three types of neurone.

12. If you were prescribed a statin drug what would be your problem?

13. Which diet focuses on eating protein and no carbohydrates?

14. Why is it necessary to vaccinate against flu every year?

15. Why isn't there a vaccine for HIV?

16. Explain what a vector is and give an example.

17. Name the two types of white blood cell that protect us from disease.
    ....

18. Explain the term 'natural immunity'.
    ....

19. Define the word homeostasis.
    ....

20. How long ago was the theory of evolution first stated?
    ....

21. What are alternative forms of a gene called?
    ....

22. Which hormones are involved in the menstrual cycle?
    ....

23. What type of organisms do we use for genetic engineering?
    ....

24. Can penicillin be used to treat measles?
    ....

25. Who developed the theory of evolution that we use today?
    ....

26. Who developed an alternative theory of evolution based on observations of giraffes?
    ....

27. A hospital patient develops the bacterial MRSA. What type of drug could be used to treat it?
    ....

28. What drugs class does cannabis belong to?
    ....

29. What is an alternative to intensive farming?
    ....

30. Where in your body would you find the chemical DNA?
    ....

Atoms and elements

Elements are made of only one type of atom.

What is in an atom?

An atom consists of a central nucleus surrounded by shells of electrons.

electrons
nucleus
an atom

How can atoms join together?

Atoms can join together by:
- sharing electrons
- giving and taking electrons

Compounds consist of two or more different types of atom that have been chemically combined.

The periodic table

Elements are often displayed in the **periodic table**. In the periodic table, elements with similar properties are found in the same vertical column. These columns are called groups.

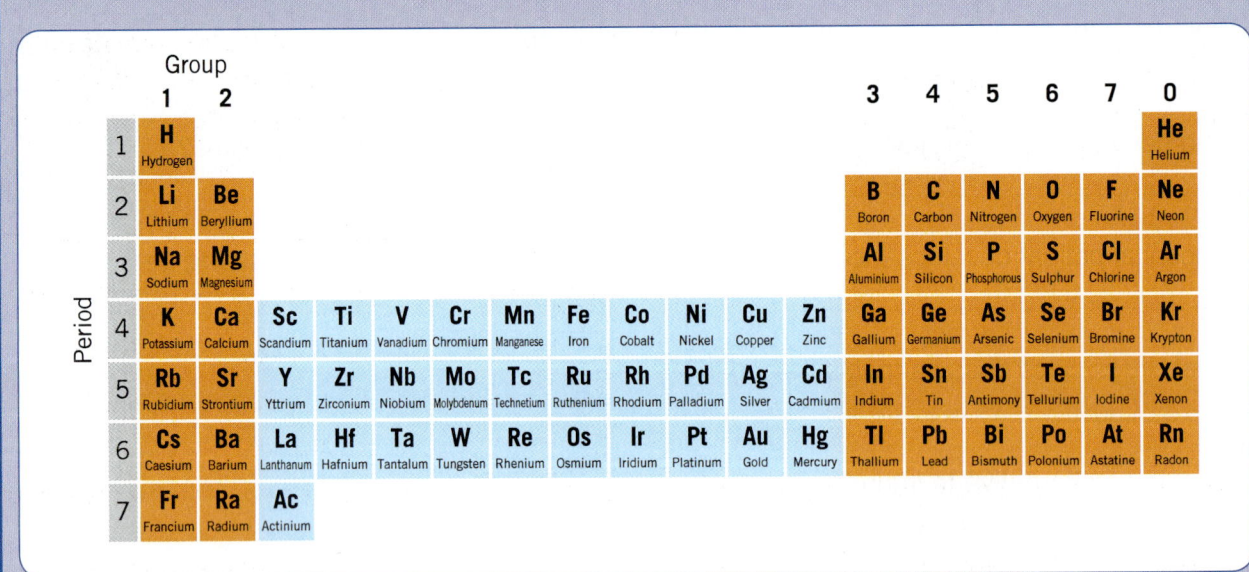

	Group 1	2											3	4	5	6	7	0
1	H Hydrogen																	He Helium
2	Li Lithium	Be Beryllium											B Boron	C Carbon	N Nitrogen	O Oxygen	F Fluorine	Ne Neon
3	Na Sodium	Mg Magnesium											Al Aluminium	Si Silicon	P Phosphorous	S Sulphur	Cl Chlorine	Ar Argon
4	K Potassium	Ca Calcium	Sc Scandium	Ti Titanium	V Vanadium	Cr Chromium	Mn Manganese	Fe Iron	Co Cobalt	Ni Nickel	Cu Copper	Zn Zinc	Ga Gallium	Ge Germanium	As Arsenic	Se Selenium	Br Bromine	Kr Krypton
5	Rb Rubidium	Sr Strontium	Y Yttrium	Zr Zirconium	Nb Niobium	Mo Molybdenum	Tc Technetium	Ru Ruthenium	Rh Rhodium	Pd Palladium	Ag Silver	Cd Cadmium	In Indium	Sn Tin	Sb Antimony	Te Tellurium	I Iodine	Xe Xenon
6	Cs Caesium	Ba Barium	La Lanthanum	Hf Hafnium	Ta Tantalum	W Tungsten	Re Rhenium	Os Osmium	Ir Iridium	Pt Platinum	Au Gold	Hg Mercury	Tl Thallium	Pb Lead	Bi Bismuth	Po Polonium	At Astatine	Rn Radon
7	Fr Francium	Ra Radium	Ac Actinium															

Symbols 1

In science, elements can be represented by **symbols**. Each element has its own unique symbol that is recognised all over the world. Each symbol consists of one or two letters and is much easier to read and write than the full name. In some cases, the symbol for an element is simply the first letter of the element's name. This letter must be a capital letter.

I

The element iodine is represented by the symbol I.

Sometimes, several elements have names that start with the same letter. When this happens, we use the first letter of the element's name together with another letter from the name. The first letter is a capital letter, the second letter is lower case.

Mg

The element magnesium is represented by the symbol Mg.

Symbols 2

Mn

The element manganese is represented by the symbol Mn.

Occasionally, an element may take its symbol from its old Latin name. When this happens, the first letter is a capital and the second letter, if there is one, is lower case.

Hg

The element mercury is represented by the symbol Hg. This comes from the Latin name for mercury which was hydrargyrum, or 'liquid silver'.

Chemical formula

A compound can be represented using a **chemical formula**.

The formula shows the type and ratio of the atoms that are joined together in the compound.

Ammonia has the chemical formula NH_3.

This shows that, in ammonia, nitrogen and hydrogen atoms are joined together in the ratio of one nitrogen atom to three hydrogen atoms.

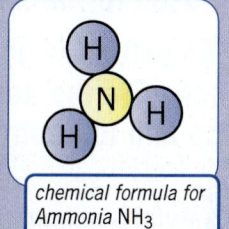

chemical formula for Ammonia NH_3

Why do we have to take care when writing symbols?

The element carbon has the symbol C.
The element oxygen has the symbol O.
The element cobalt has the symbol Co.

CO   Co CO_2

The formula CO shows that a carbon atom and an oxygen atom have been chemically combined in a one to one ratio. This is the formula of the compound carbon monoxide.

The symbol Co represents the element cobalt. Notice that the second letter of the symbol is written in lower case: if it was not, we would have a completely different substance.

The formula CO_2 shows that carbon and oxygen atoms have been chemically combined in a one to two ratio. This is the formula for the compound carbon dioxide.

As you can see, we need to be very careful when we write chemical symbols and formulae.

Chemical reactions

Symbol equations can be used to explain what happens during a chemical reaction.

When magnesium burns in air, the magnesium metal reacts with oxygen molecules to form the compound magnesium oxide. This reaction can be shown in a word equation:

Magnesium + oxygen → magnesium oxide

Or by the symbol equation:

$2Mg + O_2 \rightarrow 2MgO$

KEY TERMS

Make sure you understand these terms before moving on!
- elements
- compounds
- periodic table
- symbols
- chemical formula

QUICK TEST

1. What is the centre of an atom called?
2. What is special about elements?
3. How can atoms join together?
4. Give the chemical symbol of the element oxygen.
5. Give the chemical symbol of the element potassium.
6. Give the name of the element with the symbol Na.
7. Give the name of the element with the symbol Cr.
8. Water has the formula H_2O. Explain what this formula tells us.
9. Calcium oxide has the formula CaO. Explain what this formula tells us.
10. Sodium nitrate has the formula $NaNO_3$. Explain what this formula tells us.

ATOMS AND ELEMENTS — Chemistry

Limestone

Limestone is a *sedimentary* rock. It is mainly composed of the chemical *calcium carbonate*. It can be *quarried* and cut into blocks that can be used for *building*.

If limestone is powdered, it can be used to *neutralise* the acidity in lakes caused by acid rain and to neutralise acidic soils.

💡 *Marble is an example of a metamorphic rock. Marble is made when limestone is subjected to high pressures and temperatures. Granite is an example of an igneous rock. Igneous rocks are the hardest type of rock and metamorphic rock is harder than sedimentary rock.*

Rocks can be classified into three groups: sedimentary, metamorphic and igneous

Heating limestone

When **limestone** (calcium carbonate) is heated it breaks down to form **quicklime** (calcium oxide) and **carbon dioxide**.

calcium carbonate → calcium oxide + carbon dioxide
$CaCO_{3(s)}$ → $CaO_{(s)}$ + $CO_{2(g)}$

This is an example of a **thermal decomposition** reaction.

Quicklime (calcium oxide) reacts with water to form **slaked lime** (**calcium hydroxide**).

A solution of slaked lime is known as limewater.

calcium oxide + water → calcium hydroxide
$CaO_{(s)}$ + $H_2O_{(l)}$ → $Ca(OH)_{2(s)}$

Calcium oxide and calcium hydroxide are both **bases** so they can be used to neutralise acidic lakes and soils.

💡 *The thermal decomposition of limestone is an example of a reaction that takes in heat. This is called an endothermic reaction.*

💡 *The formula $CaCO_3$ shows us the type and ratio of atoms present. Here the calcium, carbon and oxygen atoms are present in the ratio 1:1:3.*

💡 *Calcium oxide is an example of a compound that is held together by ionic bonds. Ionic bonding involves the transfer of electrons. This forms ions with opposite charges, which then attract each other.*

Reaction summary

limestone (calcium carbonate) —heat→ carbon dioxide gas

limestone —heat→ quicklime (calcium oxide) —add water→ slaked lime (calcium hydroxide)

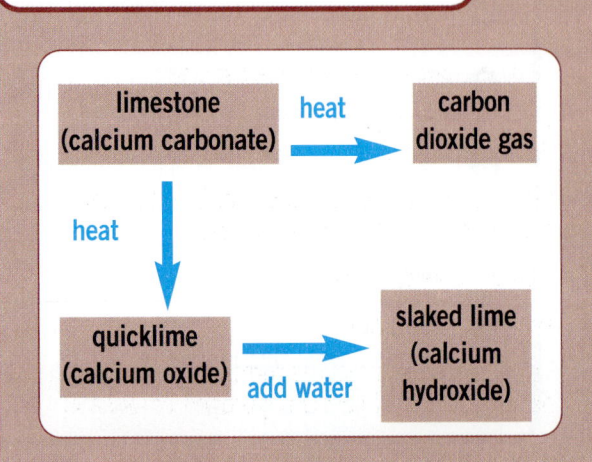

Similar thermal decomposition reactions

Other metal carbonates decompose in a **similar way** when they are heated.

When copper carbonate is heated it breaks down to give copper oxide and carbon dioxide.

copper carbonate → copper oxide + carbon dioxide
$CuCO_3$ → CuO + CO_2

Other uses of limestone

Limestone can be used to make other useful materials.

Cement
Cement is produced by roasting **powdered clay** with **powdered limestone** in a rotating kiln. It is then mixed with water and allowed to set to form the hard, stone-like material cement.

Mortar
When **water** is mixed with **cement** and **sand**, and then allowed to set, **mortar** is made.

Concrete
Concrete is made by mixing **cement**, **sand** and **rock chippings** with **water**. When water is added to cement it hydrates and binds together all the particles to form a material that is as hard as rock. Concrete is hard and cheap and is widely used in building.

Glass
Glass can be made by heating up a mixture of **limestone** (calcium carbonate), **sand** (silicon dioxide) and **soda** (sodium carbonate) until the mixture melts.

Heating baking powder

When **metal hydrogen carbonate compounds** are heated, they undergo thermal decomposition reactions to form **metal carbonates**, **carbon dioxide** and **water**.

The main chemical compound in baking powder is sodium hydrogen carbonate, $NaHCO_3$. When heated fiercely it reacts to form sodium carbonate, carbon dioxide and water.

sodium hydrogen carbonate → sodium carbonate + carbon dioxide + water

$$2NaHCO_3 \rightarrow Na_2CO_3 + CO_2 + H_2O$$

KEY TERMS
Make sure you understand these terms before moving on!
- quicklime
- thermal decomposition
- slaked lime
- cement
- mortar
- concrete
- glass

QUICK TEST
1. What is the main chemical in limestone?
2. What type of rock is limestone?
3. What type of rock is granite?
4. What is powdered limestone used for?
5. Give the word equation for the thermal decomposition of zinc carbonate.
6. What is the symbol equation for the thermal decomposition of zinc carbonate?
7. How is cement made?
8. How is glass made?
9. Name the three products formed by the thermal decomposition of sodium hydrogen carbonate.

Fuels

Fuels are burnt to release energy. In this country, the fossil fuels *coal*, *oil* and *gas* are widely used. The burning of fuel is an exothermic reaction.

Formation of coal, oil and gas

Fossil fuels are formed over **millions of years** from the fossilised remains of dead plants and animals. When plants and animals died, they fell to the sea or swamp floor. Occasionally, the remains were covered by sediment very quickly. In the absence of oxygen, the remains did not decay. Over time, more layers of sediment gradually built up and the lower layers became heated and pressurised. Over millions of years, coal, oil and natural gas are formed. Fossil fuels are non-renewable. This means that, though they take millions of years to form, they are being used up very quickly.

> Coal is mainly carbon. Petrol, diesel and oil are hydrocarbons.

Crude oil

Like many natural substances, crude oil is a **mixture of many substances**, the most important of which are called **hydrocarbons**. Hydrocarbons are molecules that only contain carbon and hydrogen atoms.

Some of the hydrocarbons have very short chains of carbon atoms. These hydrocarbons:

- are runny
- are easy to ignite
- have low boiling points
- are valuable fuels.

Other hydrocarbon molecules have much longer chains of carbon atoms. These hydrocarbons:

- are more **viscous** (less runny)
- are harder to ignite
- have higher boiling points.

These longer hydrocarbon molecules are less useful as fuels. Before any of these hydrocarbon molecules can be used, however, they must first be separated into groups of molecules with a similar number of carbon atoms called **fractions**.

> In compounds, the atoms of two or more different elements are chemically combined. In mixtures, two or more different elements or compounds are simply mixed together. Each constituent part of the mixture has its original chemical properties. This makes it quite easy to separate mixtures.

Fractional distillation of crude oil 1

Crude oil can be separated by **fractional distillation**. First the crude oil is heated until it evaporates. As the diagram of the fractionating column shows, the bottom of the column is much hotter than the top of the column. This means that short hydrocarbon molecules can reach the top of the column before they condense and are collected. Longer hydrocarbon molecules condense at higher temperatures and are collected at different points down the column.

No. carbon atoms in hydrogen chain	Temperature	Fraction collected
3	less than 40°C	refinery gas
8	40°C	petrol
10	110°C	naphtha
15	180°C	kerosene
20	250°C	diesel
35	340°C	oil
50+	above 340°C	bitumen

Fractional distillation of crude oil 2

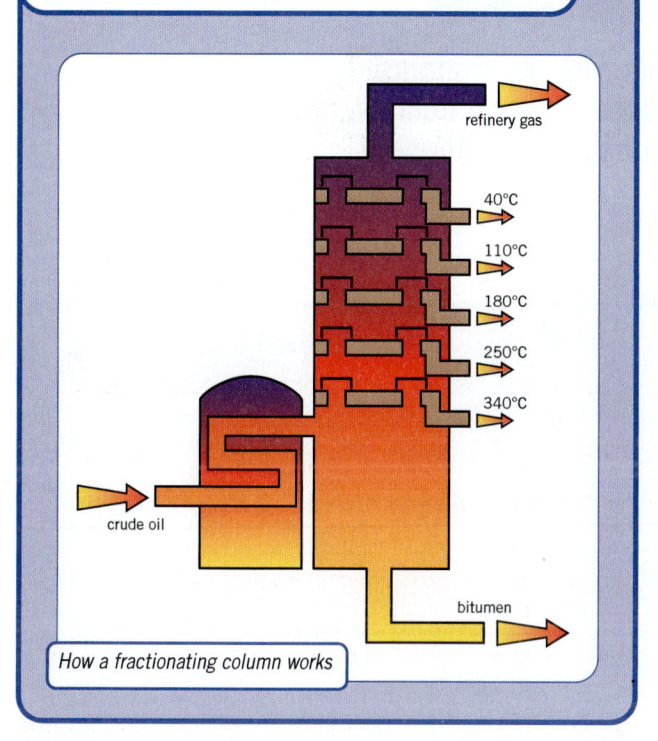

How a fractionating column works

- refinery gas
- 40°C
- 110°C
- 180°C
- 250°C
- 340°C
- crude oil
- bitumen

Cracking

The large hydrocarbon molecules separated during the fractional distillation of crude oil are not very useful. These hydrocarbon molecules, however, can be broken down into smaller, more useful and more valuable molecules by a process called **cracking**.

Cracking large hydrocarbon molecules can produce more useful products. Some of these molecules are used as fuels

Industrial cracking

The cracking of long chain hydrocarbons is carried out on a large scale. First, the long hydrocarbon molecules are heated until they evaporate, then the vapour is passed over a hot aluminium oxide catalyst.

In this example, decane is being cracked to produce octane and ethene.

Octane is one of the hydrocarbon molecules in petrol.

Ethene, which is a member of the alkene family of hydrocarbons, is also produced. Ethene is used to make a range of new compounds including plastics and industrial alcohol.

> *Cracking is an example of a thermal decomposition reaction. Some of the products of the cracking are very useful fuels.*

decane $C_{10}H_{22}$ (from the naphtha fraction) → octane C_8H_{18} + ethene C_2H_4

Cracking large hydrocarbon molecules can produce more useful products. Some of these molecules are used as fuels

KEY TERMS

Make sure you understand these terms before moving on!
- hydrocarbons
- viscous
- fractions
- fractional distillation
- cracking

QUICK TEST

1. Name three fossil fuels.
2. How long does it take for fossil fuels to form?
3. Which elements are found in hydrocarbon molecules?
4. Give three properties of short chain hydrocarbon molecules.
5. Which hydrocarbons make the best fuels?
6. Where are the short chain hydrocarbon molecules collected in a fractionating column?

Organic families

Carbon atoms have the ability to form *four bonds* with other atoms. This means that carbon atoms can be made into a large range of compounds. These compounds are the basis of life and the chemistry of these compounds is called *organic chemistry*.

Alkanes

The **alkanes** are a family of **hydrocarbon molecules**. This means that alkanes only contain hydrogen and carbon atoms. Scientists describe alkanes as **saturated** hydrocarbons because they contain no C=C bonds, so they already contain the maximum number of hydrogen atoms.

Alkanes are useful fuels, but as they do not contain C=C bonds, they do not react with bromine water.

! Alkanes have the general formula C_nH_{2n+2}

Name	methane	ethane	propane	butane
Chemical formula	CH_4	C_2H_6	C_3H_8	C_4H_{10}
Structure	H–C–H with H above and below	H–C–C–H with H's	H–C–C–C–H with H's	H–C–C–C–C–H with H's

Alkenes

The **alkenes** are also hydrocarbon molecules. Scientists describe alkenes as **unsaturated** hydrocarbons because they all contain one or more C=C bond(s).

Alkenes are more reactive than alkanes due to the presence of C=C bonds. This also means that alkenes are more useful because they can be used to make new substances. Alkenes also react with **bromine water**. Bromine water decolourises in the presence of alkenes.

! Alkenes have the general formula C_nH_{2n}

unsaturated hydrocarbons

orange brown — bromine water → colourless

Name	ethene	propene
Chemical formula	C_2H_4	C_3H_6
Structure	H₂C=CH₂	H₂C=CH–CH₃

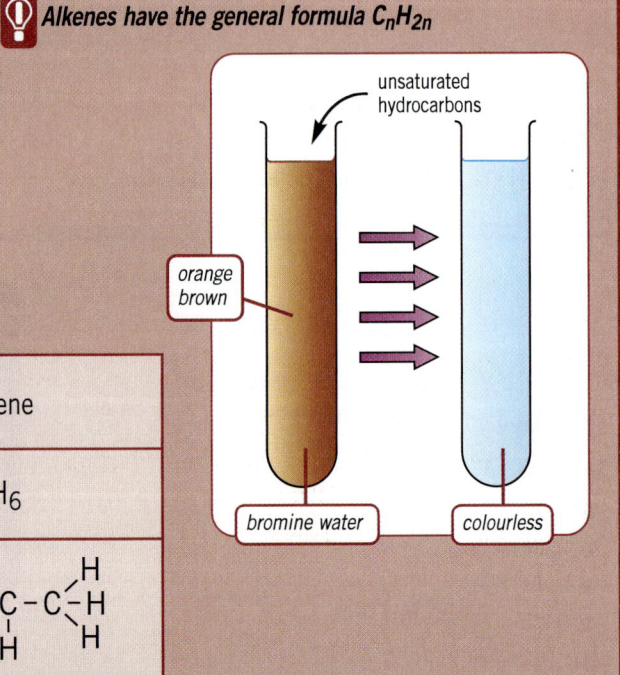

Alcohols

The term 'alcohol' is often used for the compound **ethanol**. In fact, ethanol is just one member of a family of organic compounds called alcohols. All alcohols have an **–OH** group. Each member of the family differs from the previous one by the addition of a CH_2 group.

Name	methanol	ethanol
Chemical formula	CH_3OH	C_2H_5OH
Structure	H–C(H)(H)–O–H	H–C(H)(H)–C(H)(H)–O–H

Covalent bonding

These compounds all contain covalent bonds. Covalent bonding involves the sharing of electrons. The shared pairs of electrons hold the atoms together.

Carboxylic acids

Carboxylic acids are a family of organic compounds with the functional group –COOH. Carboxylic acids are weak acids which react with metals, alkalis and carbohydrates. They have rather unpleasant smells. The well-known carboxyilic acid, ethanoic acid is found in vinegar.

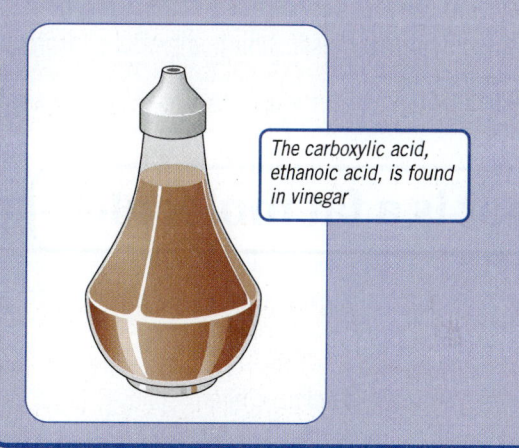

The carboxylic acid, ethanoic acid, is found in vinegar

KEY TERMS

Make sure you understand these terms before moving on!
- carbon
- alkanes
- saturated
- alkenes
- unsaturated

QUICK TEST

1. How many bonds do carbon atoms form?
2. Why are alkanes described as saturated hydrocarbons?
3. What is the name of the first member of the alkane family?
4. Draw the structure of the first four members of the alkane family.
5. Draw the structure of the first two members of the alkene family.
6. To which family does ethene belong?
7. How could you differentiate between an alkane and an alkene?
8. What is the general formula for an alkane?
9. Which hydrocarbon family does the compound ethanol belong to?
10. What is the formula of ethanol?

ORGANIC FAMILIES — Chemistry

45

Vegetable oils

Plant oils are a valuable source of *energy* in our diets. They are also essential sources of vitamins A and D.

Vegetable oils

Vegetable oils can be produced from the **fruits**, **seeds** or **nuts** of some plants.

Popular vegetable oils include olive oil and sunflower oil.

Vegetable oils can be extracted from the fruits, seeds and nuts of some plants. The oil is removed by crushing up the plant material and then collecting the oil

Fuels

When vegetable oils are burnt, they release lots of energy. In fact, vegetable oils can be used in place of fossil fuels in the production of bio-diesel. This is an alternative to normal diesel, which is produced from the fossil fuel, crude oil.

Using fats for cooking

Fats have **higher boiling points** than water, so cooking food by frying is much faster than cooking food by boiling. In addition, frying foods produces interesting **new flavours** and **increases the energy content** of the food.

Frying potatoes to make chips

What is a fat molecule?

Fats and oils are complex molecules.

Saturated and unsaturated fats
Animal fats are usually **solid**, or nearly solid, at room temperature. A saturated fat contains many C–C bonds but **no C=C** bonds. Scientists believe that people who eat lots of saturated fats may develop raised blood cholesterol levels and this is linked with an increased risk of heart disease.

Most vegetable fats are liquids at room temperature and so they are described as oils.

Animal fats

Vegetable oils contain C=C bonds. Scientists describe these molecules as unsaturated fats because they could hold more hydrogen atoms. The presence of the C=C bonds affects the way that the fatty acids in the molecule can pack together. C=C bonds are rigid and their presence causes kinks so that the fatty acids cannot pack closely together. Unsaturated fats have **lower melting points** than saturated fats. While most vegetable fats are **liquid at room temperature**, most animal fats are solids.

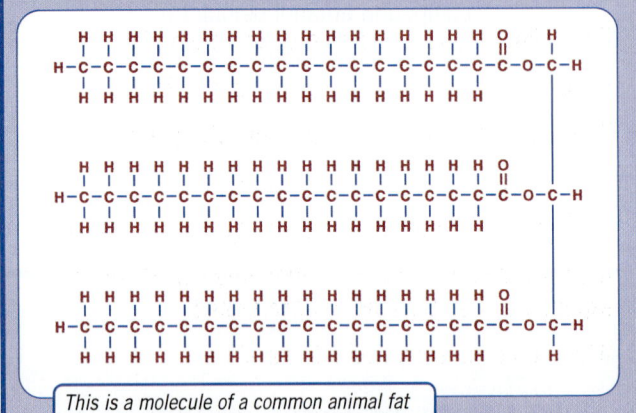

This is a molecule of a common animal fat

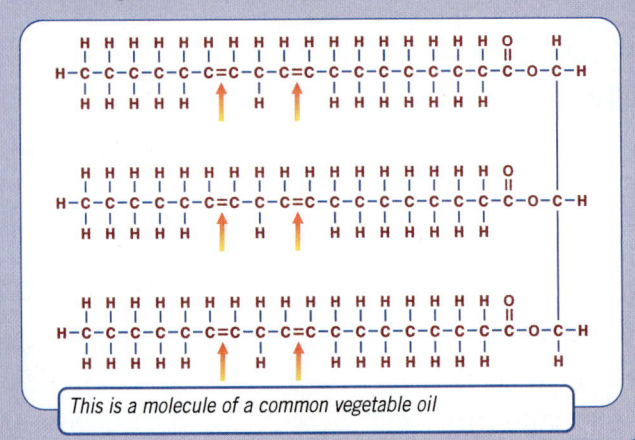

This is a molecule of a common vegetable oil

Polyunsaturated fats

Some unsaturated fats have just one C=C bond in the fatty acid chain. These are described as monounsaturated fats.

Other unsaturated fats have **many C=C bonds**. These are known as **polyunsaturated fats**. Scientists believe that polyunsaturated fats are better for people's health.

Scientists can identify an unsaturated hydrocarbon by reacting the compound with bromine water. If the compound is unsaturated and contains double bonds, the bromine water decolourises.

Emulsions

Salad dressing is an example of a type of everyday mixture called an **emulsion**. It is a **mixture of two liquids**: oil and vinegar. Salad dressing is made by shaking oil and vinegar so that they mix together. After a short while, however, the oil and vinegar **separate out to form two distinct layers**. Many of the salad dressings bought from shops contain molecules called emulsifiers that help the oil and vinegar to mix together. Emulsifiers are molecules that have two very different ends. One end is attracted to oil (hydrophobic), while the other end is attracted to the water in the vinegar (hydrophilic). The addition of emulsifiers keeps the two liquids mixed together.

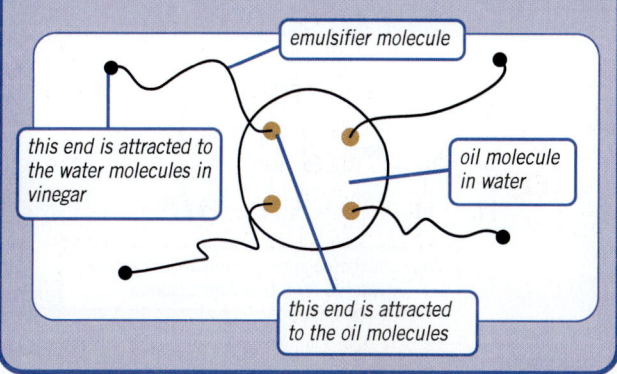

- emulsifier molecule
- this end is attracted to the water molecules in vinegar
- oil molecule in water
- this end is attracted to the oil molecules

Hydrogenated vegetable oils

Vegetable oils are often liquids at room temperature because they contain C=C bonds. There are, however, advantages to using fats that are solid at room temperature. They are easier to spread and can be used to make new products, like cakes and pastries.

Vegetable oils can be made solid at room temperature by a process known as **hydrogenation**. The oils are heated with **hydrogen and a nickel catalyst**. The hydrogen atoms add across double bonds to form fats that are solid at room temperature.

Margarine is one example of a hydrogenated vegetable oil

Food additives

Scientists often add chemicals to foods to improve them. The chemicals that have passed safety tests and are approved for use throughout the European Union are called '**E-numbers**'. They include:

- Emulsifiers, which help ingredients to mix together.
- Colours, which are added to make food look more attractive. Artificial colours can be detected using chromatography.
- Flavours, which are added to enhance taste.
- Artificial sweeteners, which are used to decrease the amount of sugar used.

VEGETABLE OILS — Chemistry

KEY TERMS
Make sure you understand these terms before moving on!
- fossil fuels
- bio-diesel
- saturated
- unsaturated
- hydrogenation
- emulsions
- E-numbers

QUICK TEST
1. From which parts of plants can we obtain oils?
2. Which part of a sunflower is used to obtain oil?
3. Which vitamins do we obtain from eating fats?
4. Why is frying food faster than boiling food?
5. Which food will contain more energy, fried or boiled?
6. If a fat is a solid at room temperature would you expect it to be saturated or unsaturated?
7. What do polyunsaturated fats have?

Plastics

Lots of small molecules can be joined together to make one big molecule.

Polymerisation

We have seen how the simplest alkene, **ethene**, can be formed by the cracking of large hydrocarbon molecules. If ethene is heated under pressure in the presence of a catalyst, many ethene molecules join together to form a larger molecule called poly(ethene) or **polythene**. Here we see how a large number of ethene molecules join together to form polythene.

The small starting molecules, in this case the ethene molecules, are called **monomers**. The C=C bonds in the ethene molecules join together to form long chain molecules called **polymers**. A polymer, therefore, is made from lots of monomer units: in fact, 'poly' means 'lots'. This is an example of an addition polymerisation reaction.

The ethene molecules have simply joined together.

Notice the 'n' at the start of the equation and the section of the polymer surrounded by brackets. The 'n' represents the number of molecules involved. The brackets are used because it would be impractical to write out the complete structure. The brackets surround a representative unit, which is then repeated through the whole polymer

Other polymers

Polymerisation reactions may involve other monomer units. The exact properties of the polymer formed depend upon:

- the monomers involved
- the conditions under which it was made.

'Slime' can be made from polyethanol. You may have seen this polymer in your science lessons.

Polypropene

Polypropene is made by an additional polymerisation reaction between many propene molecules.

Many propene molecules join together to form polypropene

Poly vinyl chloride (PVC)

Poly vinyl chloride is made by an additional polymerisation reaction between **many chloroethene** molecules.

Chloroethene used to be called vinyl chloride.

Many chloroethene (vinyl chloride) molecules join together to form poly vinyl chloride

Polytetrafluoroethene (PTFE or Teflon)

Polytetrafluoroethene is made by an additional polymerisation reaction between **many tetrafluoroethene** molecules.

Many tetrafluoroethene molecules join together to form polytetrafluoroethene (PTFE)

New polymers

Scientists are **developing new and exciting polymers**.

Hydrogels are an example of these new types of polymers. They are able to bind water and are being used to make special wound dressings to help injured people. Hydrogels help to:

- stop fluid loss from the wound
- absorb bacteria and odour molecules
- cool and cushion the wound
- reduce the number of times the wound has to be disturbed. (The hydrogel is transparent so doctors and nurses can monitor the wound without having to remove the dressing.)

Uses of plastics

Polythene
Polythene is cheap and strong.

It is used to make plastic bags and bottles.

PVC
PVC is rigid and can be used to make building materials such as drainpipes.

Chemicals called plasticisers can be added to PVC to make products like wellington boots and mackintoshes.

Polypropene
Polypropene is strong and has a high elasticity.

It is used for crates and ropes.

Polystyrene
Polystyrene is cheap and can be moulded into different shapes.

It is used for packaging and for plastic casings.

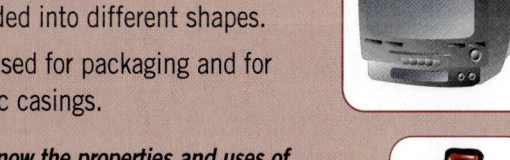

> Know the properties and uses of different plastics.

Scientific process

The problems caused by plastics that do not break down in the environment have encouraged scientists to design new biodegradable plastics.

KEY TERMS
- ethene
- polythene
- monomers
- polymers
- hydrogels

QUICK TEST

1. Draw a diagram to show how polythene is formed from ethene.
2. Draw a diagram to show how polypropene is formed from propene.
3. What type of reaction is involved in the formation of polythene?
4. What is the name given to the small units that join together to form a polymer?
5. What is the old name for chloroethene?
6. What is the trade name for polytetrafluroethene?
7. Name a new polymer that is used to make wound dressings?
8. Which plastic is cheap and strong?
9. Which plastic has high elasticity?
10. Which plastic is used to make milk crates?

49

Ethanol

Ethanol is a member of the alcohol family of organic compounds.

Uses of ethanol

Ethanol has the structure:

The structure of ethanol

Ethanol is found in drinks like beer and wine, however, in large amounts, it is toxic. Ethanol has many useful properties. It is a **good solvent** and evaporates quickly. Many aftershaves contain ethanol. Ethanol is an important raw material and can also be used as a **fuel**.

Methanol is another member of the alcohol group and is even more toxic than ethanol. If someone drank methanol, they could become blind or even die. Methylated spirit is a mixture of methanol, ethanol and a purple dye. The purple dye is there to warn people about its toxicity and the unpleasant taste of methylated spirit is there to try to stop people from drinking it.

Ethanol as a fuel

In some countries, alcohol is made from sugar-beet or sugar-cane. This alcohol can then be mixed with petrol to produce a fuel for vehicles like cars. Ethanol is a renewable energy resource that burns very cleanly. **Alcohols**, however, **release less energy** than petrol when they are burnt. In order to produce enough alcohol for fuel, large areas of fertile land would be required to grow the plants needed to produce the alcohol.

Sugar-cane can be used to produce alcohol, which can be burnt as a fuel

Fermentation

Fermentation has been used to make alcohol for thousands of years. We use fermentation to make alcoholic drinks. Fruits, vegetables and cereals are all sources of the sugar, glucose, $C_6H_{12}O_6$.

During fermentation, **yeast** is used to catalyse (speed up) the reaction in which glucose is converted into ethanol and carbon dioxide.

$$\text{glucose} \xrightarrow{\text{yeast}} \text{ethanol} + \text{carbon dioxide}$$
$$C_6H_{12}O_6 \rightarrow 2C_2H_5OH + 2CO_2$$

The temperature of the reaction has to be carefully controlled. If the temperature falls too low, the yeast becomes inactive and the rate of the reaction slows down. If the temperature rises too high, the yeast is denatured and stops working altogether.

Ethanol produced by fermentation, has a concentration of around 6 to 14%. Some people prefer drinks with higher alcohol content. These higher concentrations of alcohol are achieved by **fractional distillation**.

There is a very strong link between the consumption of alcohol and an increased risk of accidents and raised crime levels. Some religions prohibit the consumption of all alcoholic drinks altogether.

> *Yeast is an enzyme or biological catalyst. It speeds up the conversion of sugar to alcohol and carbon dioxide, but yeast is not used up in the process.*

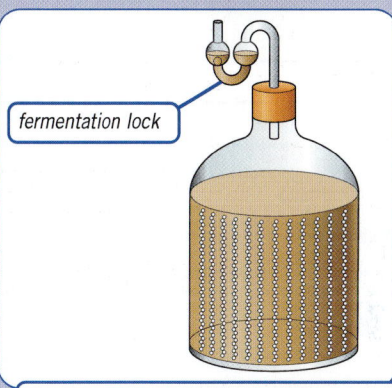

The fermentation lock allows carbon dioxide to escape, but stops oxygen in the air from reaching the alcohol. This is important, as ethanol can be easily oxidised to ethanoic acid, which would make the drink taste sour

Industrial alcohol

There is another, more modern way of producing vast amounts of alcohol. During this method, **ethene** (which is produced during the cracking of long chain hydrocarbons) is **reacted with steam to produce ethanol**.

$$\text{ethene} + \text{steam} \rightarrow \text{ethanol}$$
$$C_2H_4 + H_2O \rightarrow C_2H_5OH$$

A catalyst of **phosphoric acid and a temperature of 300°C** are needed.

This method of producing ethanol is much cheaper than fermentation. However, our reserves of fossil fuels are finite and will run out one day.

KEY TERMS

Make sure you understand these terms before moving on!
- solvent
- alcohol
- renewable
- fermentation
- yeast

QUICK TEST

1. What is the formula of ethanol?
2. Give three uses of ethanol.
3. What could happen to someone who drinks the alcohol methanol?
4. What is added to methylated spirit to stop people from drinking it?
5. What is the catalyst used in fermentation?
6. What is the formula of glucose?
7. What happens to yeast if the temperature is too high?
8. What is the name of the catalyst that is used in the industrial production of ethanol?
9. What is the word equation for the industrial production of ethanol?

ETHANOL Chemistry

Evolution of the atmosphere

The composition of today's *atmosphere* is:

- about 80% nitrogen
- about 20% oxygen
- small amounts of other gases such as carbon dioxide, water vapour and noble gases, e.g. argon.

Its make-up has remained stable for the last 200 million years. This has not always been the case. Over the history of the Earth, the composition of the atmosphere has changed and *evolved*.

Formation of the atmosphere

The first billion years

During the first billion years of the Earth's life there was **enormous volcanic activity**. Volcanoes belched out carbon dioxide (CO_2), steam (H_2O), ammonia (NH_3) and methane (CH_4).

The atmosphere was **mainly carbon dioxide** and there was very little oxygen. In fact, Earth's early atmosphere was very similar to the modern day atmospheres of the planets **Mars and Venus**. The steam **condensed** to form the early oceans.

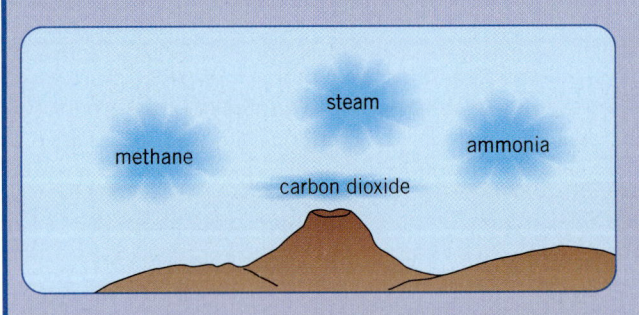

Later

During the next two billion years, **plants evolved** and began to cover the surface of the Earth.

The plants grew very well in the carbon dioxide rich atmosphere. They steadily removed carbon dioxide and produced oxygen (O_2).

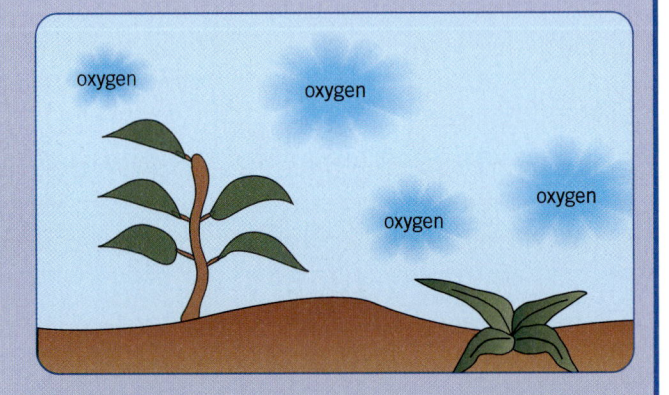

Later still

Most of the carbon from the carbon dioxide in the early atmosphere gradually became **locked up** as carbonate minerals and fossil fuels in sedimentary rocks.

The ammonia in the early atmosphere reacted with oxygen to release nitrogen. Living organisms, such as denitrifying bacteria, also produced nitrogen.

As the amount of oxygen increased, an **ozone layer** (O_3) developed. This layer filtered out harmful ultraviolet radiation from the Sun, enabling new, more complex life forms to develop.

This limestone rock is rich in the chemical calcium carbonate

Is burning fossil fuel going to cause problems?

The level of carbon dioxide in our atmosphere has increased since the Industrial Revolution as we have continuously burnt more fossil fuels. These fossil fuels have stored carbon dioxide from the Earth's early atmosphere for hundreds of millions of years.

However, the amount of carbon dioxide now being released into the atmosphere by the burning of fossil fuels is not the same as the actual increase in the amount of carbon dioxide in the atmosphere. A lot of the carbon dioxide appears to be missing. Scientists believe that much of the carbon dioxide produced is removed from the atmosphere by the **reaction between carbon dioxide and seawater**. This reaction produces:

- **insoluble carbonate** salts, which are deposited as sediment
- **soluble calcium and magnesium hydrogen carbonate** salts, which sometimes end up as sediment.

Much of the carbon dioxide is, therefore, locked up in sediment for long periods of time. Some of this carbon dioxide is later released back into the atmosphere, when the sediment is sub-ducted underground by geological activity and is released by volcanic eruption.

However, not all of the carbon dioxide released by the burning of fossil fuels is removed in these ways. Many people are concerned about rising levels of carbon dioxide in the Earth's atmosphere and the possible link between these increased levels and **global warming**.

Scientific process

Our ideas about the evolution of the Earth's atmosphere have come from scientists' studies of rocks formed in the past. Our ideas have changed as more evidence has become available.

KEY TERMS

Make sure you understand these terms before moving on!
- atmosphere
- evolved
- volcanic
- condensed
- ozone layer
- global warming

QUICK TEST

1. Roughly how much of today's atmosphere is made up of oxygen?
2. What is the main gas in the atmosphere today?
3. What other gases are present in small amounts in the Earth's atmosphere?
4. Which gases formed the Earth's early atmosphere?
5. Which was the main gas in the Earth's early atmosphere?
6. How did the evolution of plants affect the Earth's atmosphere?
7. What happened to most of the carbon dioxide in the Earth's early atmosphere?
8. What does the ozone layer do?
9. How did the development of the ozone layer affect life on Earth?
10. Why is the amount of carbon dioxide in the Earth's atmosphere increasing?

EVOLUTION OF THE ATMOSPHERE — Chemistry

Pollution of the atmosphere

The atmosphere can be polluted in many ways.

Acid rain

Fossil fuels like coal, oil and gas often contain small amounts of **sulphur**. When these fuels are burnt, the gas **sulphur dioxide**, SO_2, is produced. This gas can dissolve in rainwater to form **acid rain**. Acid rain can affect the environment by damaging statues and buildings, as well as plant and aquatic life.

Reducing acid rain

The amount of acid rain produced can be reduced in several ways. The easiest way is simply to **use less electricity**, by turning off lights when they are not in use and not leaving everyday appliances on standby mode. Alternatively, sulphur compounds can be **removed directly from oil and gas** before they are burnt so that they do not produce sulphur dioxide as they burn. In addition, the sulphur that is removed is a valuable material that can be sold.

It is more difficult to remove sulphur from the fossil fuel coal. Instead, the sulphur dioxide produced can be **removed from the waste gases** before they are released into the atmosphere. In power stations, this is done by scrubbers. The scrubbers react sulphur dioxide (from the waste gases) with calcium carbonate to produce gypsum and carbon dioxide.

Carbon monoxide

The gas carbon monoxide, CO, can also cause problems. When fossil fuels containing carbon and hydrogen are burnt, the gases carbon dioxide and water vapour are produced. However, if carbon is burnt in an **insufficient** supply of oxygen, the gas carbon monoxide can also be produced.

Carbon monoxide is colourless, odourless and very poisonous. Faulty gas appliances can produce carbon monoxide and, therefore, it is important that they are regularly serviced.

Incomplete combustion is undesirable in several ways:
1. *Carbon monoxide is produced.*
2. *Less heat than expected is given off when the fuel is burnt.*
3. *Soot is produced which must then be cleaned. (A sooty flame has a yellow colour.)*

Global dimming

Global dimming is caused by **smoke particles** that are released into the atmosphere. Scientists believe that these smoke particles reduce the amount of sunlight that reaches the Earth's surface and may even affect weather patterns.

Carbon dioxide and the greenhouse effect

The **greenhouse effect** is slowly heating up the Earth. When fossil fuels are burnt, the gas carbon dioxide is produced. Although some of this carbon dioxide is removed from the atmosphere by the reaction between carbon dioxide and seawater, the overall amount of carbon dioxide in the atmosphere has increased over the last 200 years.

The carbon dioxide gas **traps the heat energy** that has reached the Earth from the Sun. **Global warming** may mean that the polar **icecaps** will eventually melt and this could cause massive flooding.

> Carbon dioxide is the gas used by plants during photosynthesis.

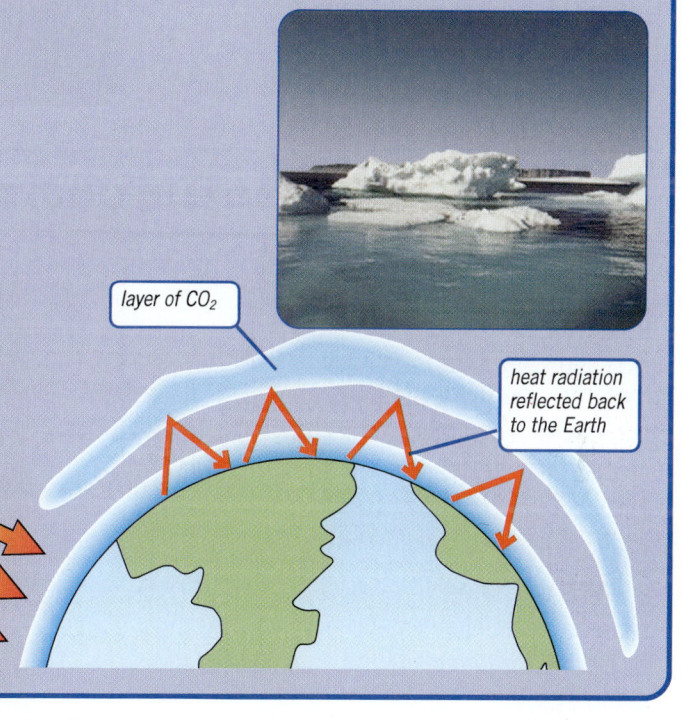

layer of CO_2

heat radiation reflected back to the Earth

light energy from the Sun

Scientific theory

Not all scientists believe that human activity is causing global warming. Other factors, such as solar cycles, may be more important. Until we have more evidence, however, we will not really know.

KEY TERMS

Make sure you understand these terms before moving on!
- acid rain
- insufficient
- global dimming
- global warming
- icecaps

POLLUTION OF THE ATMOSPHERE — Chemistry

QUICK TEST

1. What is the name of the gas produced when sulphur is burnt?
2. Which fossil fuel contains the most sulphur?
3. How can switching off lights prevent the formation of acid rain?
4. How can you tell a fuel is being burnt in a poor supply of oxygen?
5. What gas is produced when carbon is burnt in a good supply of oxygen?
6. What gas is produced when carbon is burnt in an insufficient supply of oxygen?
7. What causes global dimming?
8. What are the problems associated with global dimming?
9. Which gas is linked to the greenhouse effect?
10. Which gas is used during photosynthesis?

Pollution of the environment

All substances are obtained or made from matter from the Earth's crust, sea or atmosphere. It is vital, therefore, that we protect the environment from harmful *pollution*.

Problems with bauxite quarrying

Aluminium is extracted from its ore **bauxite**. Unfortunately, this ore is often found in environmentally sensitive areas like the Amazonian **rainforest**. Bauxite is extracted from large, open-cast mines. Every new mine means that many trees have to be cut down. Trees must also be cleared when new roads are built to give access to the mines. In addition, the area around the mine can become polluted by litter and oil.

However, aluminium can be recycled. This cuts down on landfill in Britain and helps to preserve the rainforests.

Aluminium drinks cans

Problems with limestone quarrying

Limestone is a very important raw material. However, the economic benefits of quarrying for limestone must be balanced against the social and environmental consequences of quarrying. Limestone has to be blasted from hill sides in huge quantities. This **scars the landscape, causes noise pollution and dust, and affects local wildlife**.

Transporting limestone from the quarry can also cause problems, with **heavy lorries creating noise, congestion and damaging local roads**.

However, quarrying does create new **jobs** and bring new **money** into an area.

Problems disposing of plastic

Plastics are very useful materials. They are very stable and unreactive: most plastics do not react with water, oxygen or other common chemicals. Plastics are also **non-biodegradable**, which means that micro-organisms do not decompose them.

When plastic objects are no longer needed, they do not rot away. They remain in the environment and may cause problems. Plastic objects now fill many landfill sites.

We can get rid of plastics by burning them, but this solution can also cause problems. Although some plastics burn quite easily, they can give off **harmful** gases. The common plastic PVC releases the gas hydrogen chloride when it is burnt.

In response to these problems, scientists have developed new, **biodegradable** plastics, which will eventually rot away.

KEY TERMS

Make sure you understand these terms before moving on!

- pollution
- bauxite
- non-biodegradable
- harmful
- biodegradable

QUICK TEST

1. Name the main ore of aluminium.
2. Name one place where aluminium ore can be mined.
3. How can we help cut landfill and preserve rainforests?
4. How can limestone extraction affect the landscape?
5. What are the advantages of a new, local limestone quarry?
6. How can lorries cause problems near limestone quarries?
7. Where does rubbish end up?
8. What is the name used to describe materials that are not broken down by micro-organisms?
9. What is the harmful gas produced when PVC is burnt?
10. Which plastics will break down in the environment?

POLLUTION OF THE ENVIRONMENT — Chemistry

Evidence for plate tectonics

Silicon, oxygen and aluminium are all very abundant in the Earth's crust.

Structure of the earth

Scientists believe that the Earth has a layered structure.

- The outer layer of **crust** is very thin and has a low density.
- The next layer down is called the **mantle**. This layer extends almost halfway to the centre of the Earth. The rock in the mantle is mainly solid but small amounts must be liquid because it flows very slowly.
- At the centre of the Earth is the **core**. The core has two parts: the outer core is liquid and the inner core, which is under great pressure, is solid.

Crust – the crust is the outer-most layer of the Earth, which is rich in silicon, oxygen and aluminium. The outer layer of crust is very thin and has a low density

Mantle – the mantle is found between the crust and the core. It is partially liquid. As a result, the rocks in the mantle flow slowly

Core – the core is the central part of the Earth. It is thought to be made of iron and nickel. The core has two parts. The outer core is liquid and the inner core, which is under even greater pressure than the outer core, is solid

Continental crust – mainly granite

Oceanic crust – mainly basalt

Evidence for the structure of the Earth

Evidence for the layered structure of the Earth comes from studies of the way that **seismic waves** (the shock waves sent out by earthquakes) travel through the Earth. The material that they are travelling through affects the speed of the waves. These studies show that the outer core is liquid, while the inner core is solid.

The overall density of the Earth is greater than the density of the rocks that make up the Earth's crust. This means that the rocks in the mantle and the core must be much denser than the rocks we observe in the crust. Scientists believe that the core is mainly made of **iron and nickel**.

Movement of the crust 1

People used to believe that the features of the Earth's surface, e.g. mountain ranges, were formed as the surface of the Earth shrank as it cooled down. However, scientists now believe that the Earth's geological features can be explained using a single, unifying theory called **plate tectonics**.

The scientist, Alfred Wegener, first proposed the ideas involved in plate tectonics. At first these ideas were resisted, particularly by religious groups, but as more evidence emerged, the theory of plate tectonics was gradually accepted.

The main idea in plate tectonics is that the Earth's **lithosphere** (crust and upper mantle) is split up into about 12 large plates. Each of these plates moves slowly over the Earth's surface, at a rate of just a few centimetres a

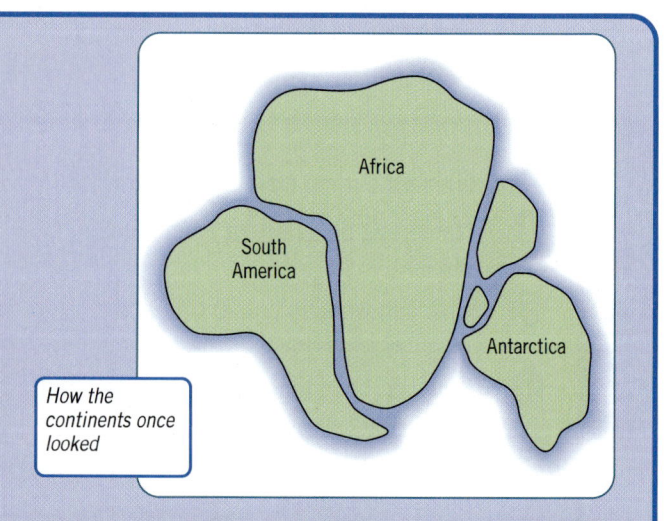

How the continents once looked

year. The movement of the plates is caused by **convection currents** in the mantle. These currents are caused by the **natural radioactive decay** of elements deep inside the Earth, which release heat energy.

Movement of the crust 2

At one time, all the continents were joined together to form a super continent called Pangea. Since that time, the continents have moved apart and are now at their maximum separation.

Evidence to support the theory of plate tectonics

There are many clues that support our ideas about plate tectonics:

1 As soon as the South American coast was mapped, people began to notice how the east coast of South America and the west coast of Africa fitted together like pieces of an enormous **jigsaw**.

2 Examination of **fossil remains** in South America and Africa showed that rocks of the same age contained the remains of an unusual, freshwater, crocodile-like creature.

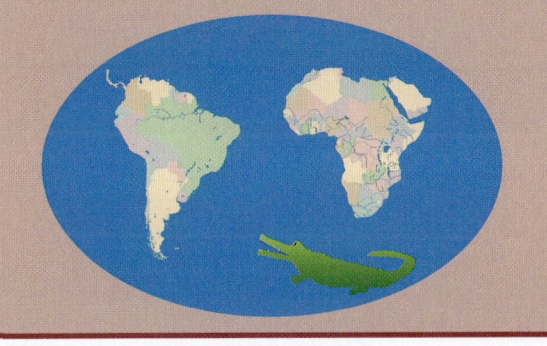

3 Further evidence that South America and Africa were once joined was found when scientists discovered that **rock strata** of the same age were strikingly similar on both sides of the Atlantic.

4 British rocks that were formed in the Carboniferous period (300 million years ago) must have formed in tropical swamps. Yet rocks found in Britain that formed 200 million years ago must have formed in deserts. This shows that Britain has travelled through **different climatic zones** as the tectonic plate that Britain rests on moved across the Earth's surface.

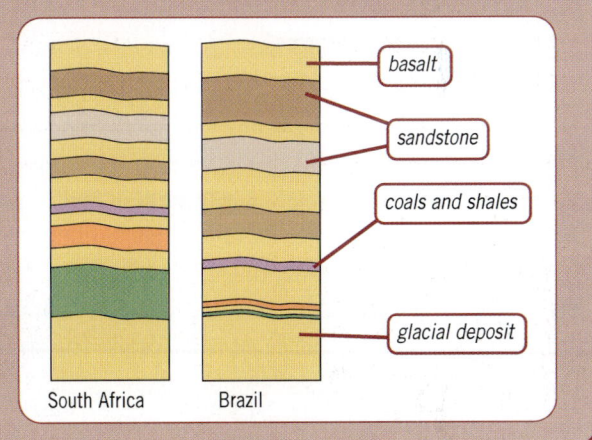

Scientific process

Our ideas about plate tectonics have changed over time. Scientists build a model that fits with the evidence that is available to them at any given time. When new evidence becomes available, scientists must re-evaluate existing models and, if necessary, change them to take in the new evidence.

KEY TERMS
- crust
- mantle
- core
- seismic waves
- plate tectonics
- convection currents

QUICK TEST

1. What name is given to the outer layer of the Earth?
2. In which state is the Earth's inner core?
3. Which elements are abundant in the Earth's crust?
4. Which elements are abundant in the Earth's core?
5. How fast do tectonic plates move?
6. What is the Earth's lithosphere?
7. Historically, how did people once believe that mountain ranges had formed?
8. What produces the heat that drives the plates' movements?

Consequences of plate tectonics

The movement of tectonic plates can cause many problems, including earthquakes and volcanoes. These problems tend to be worse near the edges of plates. These are known as the *plate boundaries*.

Plate movements

The plates can move in three different ways:
1. They can slide past each other.
2. They can move towards each other.
3. They can move away from each other.

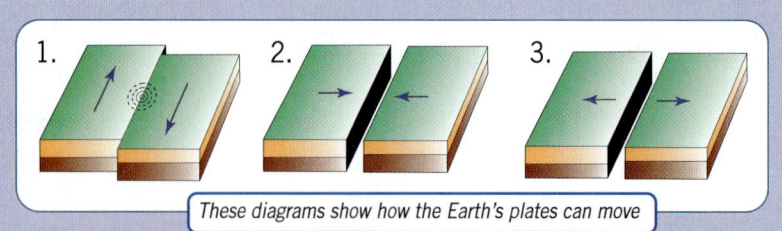

These diagrams show how the Earth's plates can move

Earthquakes

Earthquakes are caused by tectonic plates sliding past each other. The San Andreas Fault, in California, is a famous example of this occurring. The plates in this area have been fractured into a very complicated pattern. As the plates try to move past each other, they tend to stick together, rather than slide smoothly past each other. When the **plates stick together, forces build up**, until eventually the **plates move suddenly**. The strain that has built up is released as an earthquake. If this

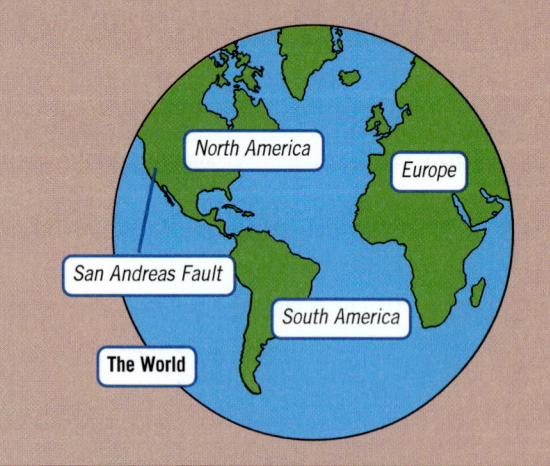

Earthquakes can cause enormous damage. This photograph was taken in Los Angeles after the 1994 earthquake

happens under the oceans, the result is catastrophic tsunami waves.

Scientists have studied earthquakes in an attempt to predict exactly when and where future earthquakes might occur, so that they can warn people to get away from the affected areas. However, with so many **factors** involved, it is not always possible to predict exactly when an earthquake will occur. When they do happen, they can cause massive destruction and loss of life.

Volcanoes 1

Volcanoes are found in locations around the Earth where two plates are moving towards each other.
- These convergent plate boundaries often involve a collision between an **oceanic and a continental plate**.
- **Oceanic plates** contain minerals that are rich in the elements iron and magnesium and they are **denser** than **continental plates**.
- When an oceanic plate and a continental plate converge, the denser, oceanic plate is forced beneath the continental plate.

Volcanoes 2

- The continental plate is stressed and the existing rocks are folded and metamorphosed.
- As the oceanic plate is forced down below the continental plate, seawater lowers the melting point of the rock and some of the oceanic plate may melt to form magma. This magma can rise up through cracks to form volcanoes. 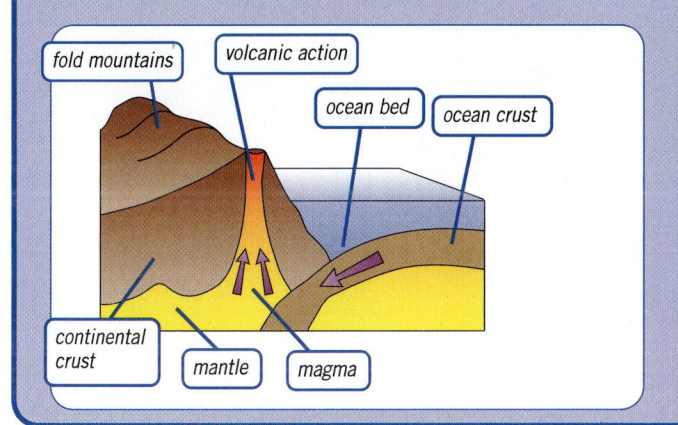
- As the plates are also moving past each other, earthquakes are common in these areas too.
- A convergent plate boundary along the Western coast of South America caused the Andes mountain range.

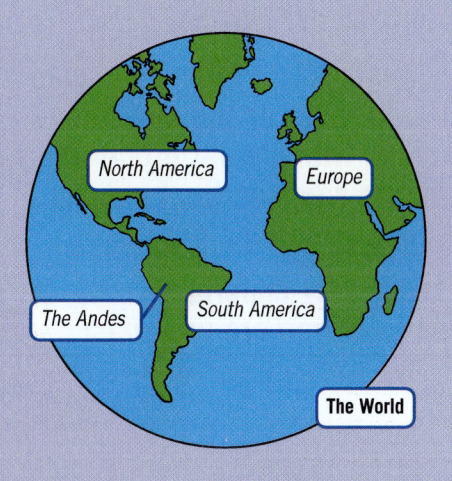

Mid ocean ridge basalts

Another consequence of plate tectonics is the formation of mid ocean ridge basalts.

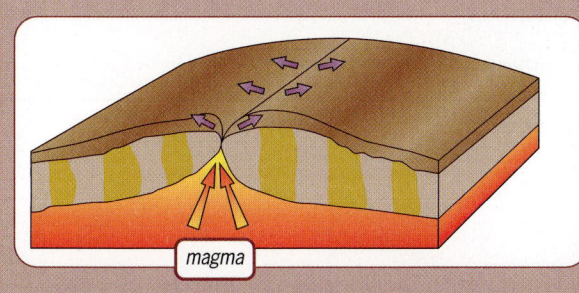

When tectonic plates move apart, magma rises to the surface. This usually occurs under oceans. As the molten rock cools, it solidifies and forms the igneous rock **basalt**. In fact, these plate boundaries are often referred to as 'constructive plate boundaries' because new crust is being made.

Basalt is rich in iron, which is magnetic. As the basalt cools down, **the iron rich minerals in the basalt line up with the Earth's magnetic field**. By examining the direction in which these minerals have lined up, scientists are able to work out the direction of the Earth's magnetic field. However, examination of the basalt rocks on either side of a mid ocean ridge reveal a **striped magnetic reversal pattern**. The pattern is symmetrical about the ridge and is evidence that, periodically, the Earth's magnetic field changes direction. This reversal appears to be very sudden and to occur about every half a million years. According to the rock record another reversal is now long overdue!

QUICK TEST

1. What are the three ways that plates can move?
2. How are earthquakes caused?
3. Why can't scientists predict the exact date of an earthquake?
4. Where is the San Andreas Fault?
5. Which type of plate is densest?
6. How is magma formed when two plates converge?
7. Why do earthquakes sometimes occur near volcanoes?
8. Which element is abundant in basalt?
9. What affects the iron rich minerals in basalt?

KEY TERMS

- plate boundaries
- earthquakes
- factors
- volcanoes
- oceanic plates
- continental plates
- basalt

CONSEQUENCES OF PLATE TECTONICS — Chemistry

Extraction of iron

Iron is an element. Elements are substances that are made of only one type of atom.

There are only about 100 different elements. Elements are often displayed on the periodic table. In the periodic table, elements with similar properties are found in the same vertical column. These columns are called groups.

Iron is an extremely important metal. It is extracted from iron ore in a *blast furnace*.

Fe
Iron

Atomic symbol for iron

Methods of extraction

The more reactive a metal is, the harder it is to remove from its compound. Gold is so unreactive that it is found uncombined. However, all other metals are found in compounds. Occasionally we may find rocks that contain metals in such high concentrations that it is economically worthwhile to extract the metal from the rock. Such rocks are called **ores**. The method chosen to extract the metal depends on the **reactivity** of the metal.

Iron is less reactive than carbon. Iron can be extracted from iron oxide by reducing the metal oxide with carbon.

potassium sodium calcium magnesium aluminium	metals that are more reactive than carbon are extracted by **electrolysis**
carbon zinc iron tin lead gold	metals that are less reactive than carbon are extracted by reducing the metal oxide using **carbon** (or carbon monoxide)

The solid raw materials

The solid raw materials in the blast furnace are:
- iron ore
- **coke** (which is a source of the element carbon)
- **limestone** (which reacts with impurities).

The main ore of iron is **haematite**. This ore contains the compound iron (III) oxide, Fe_2O_3.

What happens in the blast furnace?

1. Hot air is blasted into the furnace. The oxygen in the air reacts with the carbon in the coke to form carbon dioxide and release energy.

> carbon + oxygen → carbon dioxide
> $C_{(s)}$ + $O_{2(g)}$ → $CO_{2(g)}$

2. At the very high temperatures inside the blast furnace, carbon dioxide reacts with more carbon to form carbon monoxide.

> carbon dioxide + carbon → carbon monoxide
> $CO_{2(g)}$ + $C_{(s)}$ → $2CO_{(g)}$

3. The carbon monoxide reacts with iron oxide to form iron and carbon dioxide.

> carbon monoxide + iron oxide → iron + carbon dioxide
> $3CO_{(g)}$ + $Fe_2O_{3(s)}$ → $2Fe_{(l)}$ + $3CO_{2(g)}$

During this reaction:

- the iron oxide is reduced to iron
- the carbon monoxide is oxidised to carbon dioxide

Due to the high temperatures in the blast furnace, the iron that is made is in liquid form. This molten iron is **dense** and sinks to the bottom of the furnace where it can be removed.

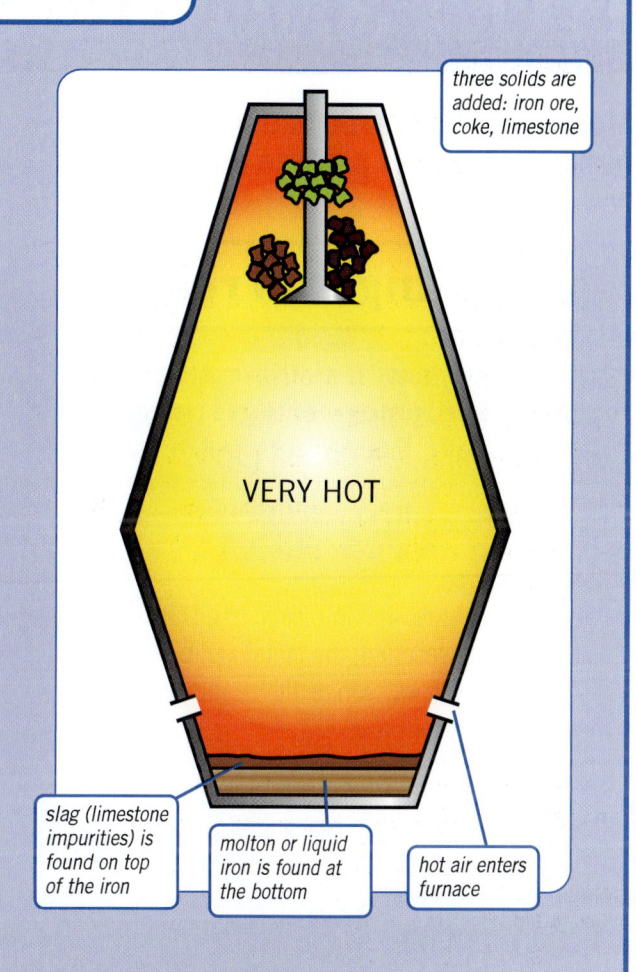

Diagram labels: three solids are added: iron ore, coke, limestone; VERY HOT; slag (limestone impurities) is found on top of the iron; molton or liquid iron is found at the bottom; hot air enters furnace

💡 *Iron ore is mainly reduced by the gas carbon monoxide.*

Removing impurities in the blast furnace

Haematite (iron ore) contains many impurities: most commonly it contains substantial amounts of silicon dioxide (silica). Limestone is added to the blast furnace because it reacts with these silica impurities to form **slag**. Slag has a low density and so it floats to the top of the iron ore, where it can be removed. The slag can be used in road building and in the manufacture of fertilisers.

KEY TERMS
- blast furnace
- extraction
- ores
- reactivity
- coke
- limestone
- dense

QUICK TEST

1. Which element is so unreactive that it can be found uncombined?
2. Which method of extraction can be used for metals that are less reactive than carbon?
3. Which method of extraction can be used for metals that are more reactive than carbon?
4. What is the name of the main ore of iron?
5. What are the three solid raw materials added to the blast furnace?
6. What is the other raw material used in the blast furnace?
7. Which gas actually reduces iron oxide to iron?
8. Why does iron sink to the bottom of the furnace?
9. What is the name of the substance formed when limestone reacts with silica?
10. How can this substance be used?

EXTRACTION OF IRON — Chemistry

Iron and steel

Most of the iron made in the blast furnace is used to produce *steel*.

Preventing iron rusting

Iron **corrodes** or 'rusts' faster than most transition metals. However, rusting requires the presence of both oxygen and water. If we can completely remove either of these chemicals we can stop the iron from **rusting**. This can be done in several ways.

Coating the iron
Painting or coating iron in plastic or oil can stop **oxygen and water** from reaching the metal and prevent it rusting. However, as soon as the coating is damaged the iron will start to rust.

Sacrificial protection
Sacrificial protection involves a different approach. We can stop iron from rusting by placing it in contact with a more reactive metal like **zinc or magnesium**. The iron is protected because the more reactive metal reacts, instead of the iron. For this reason, this method is called sacrificial protection. Expensive objects made from iron, such as speedboat engines, are protected in this way.

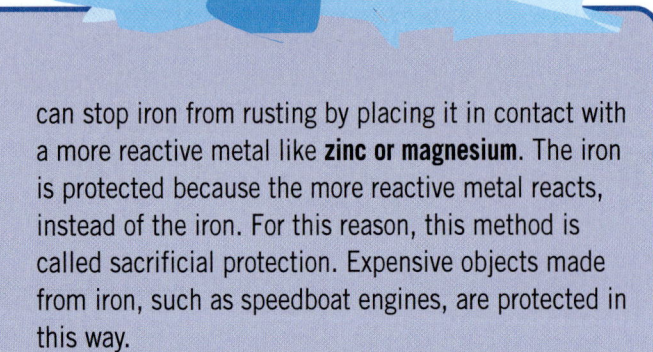

Alloying the metal
Iron can also be protected by mixing the metal with other metals and carbon to form **alloys** such as stainless steel.

Cast iron

The iron that is made in a blast furnace contains large amounts of the element carbon. If this iron is allowed to cool down and solidify it forms cast iron. **Cast iron** contains about 96% pure iron. This metal can be used to make objects like drain covers. It is:

- hard
- strong
- does not rust.

Cast iron does have one notable disadvantage: it is brittle and can easily crack.

Drain covers need to be strong and must not rust. They are made from cast iron

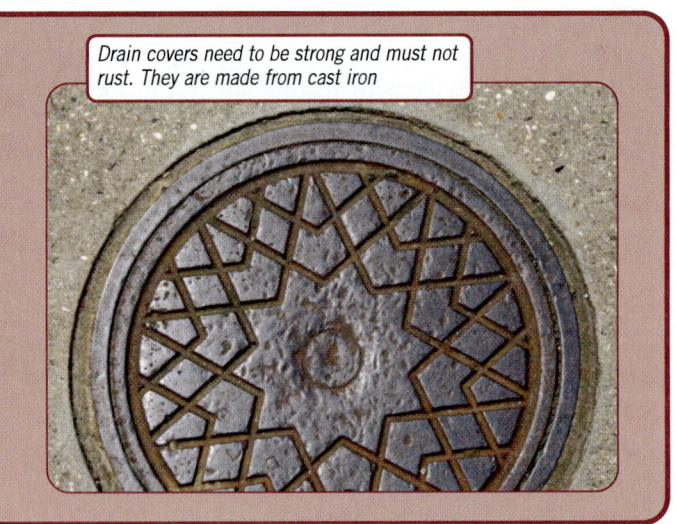

Wrought iron

Wrought iron is made by removing the impurities from cast iron. Wrought iron is much softer than cast iron and can be used to make objects like gates.

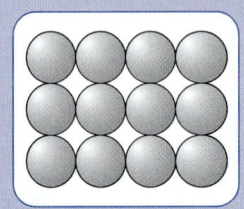

Wrought iron is softer than cast iron because of its structure. It is made from almost pure iron. This means that the iron atoms form a **very regular arrangement**. The layers of iron atoms are able to slip easily over each other. This makes wrought iron soft and easy to shape.

This beautiful gate is made from wrought iron. Wrought iron is much softer than cast iron

Steel

Most iron is made into steel. Most of the metal objects that we use today are made from steel.
- First, the carbon impurities are removed from iron to produce pure iron.
- Then other metals, and carefully controlled amounts of the non-metal element carbon, are added to the iron.

Steel is much harder than wrought iron because it consists of atoms of different elements. These atoms are different sizes. This means that the atoms in steel cannot pack together to form a regular structure. This irregular structure makes it **very difficult for the layers of atoms to slide** over each other and makes steel hard.

Designer steels

By carefully controlling the amount of carbon that is added to steel, scientists can produce a steel that has exactly the right properties for each particular job.

Low carbon steels are:
- soft
- easy to shape

Objects such as car bodies are made from low carbon steels.

Medium carbon steels are:
- harder
- stronger
- less easy to shape

Objects such as hammers are made from medium carbon steels.

High carbon steels are:
- hard
- strong
- brittle
- difficult to shape

Objects such as razor blades are made from high carbon steels.

We can also alloy iron with other metals to form different types of steel.

Stainless steel

Stainless steel is a very widely used **alloy**. It consists of:
- 70% iron
- 20% chromium
- 10% nickel

Stainless steel is extremely resistant to corrosion.

KEY TERMS

Make sure you understand these terms before moving on!
- steel
- corrodes
- rusting
- sacrificial protection
- alloys
- cast iron
- wrought iron
- stainless steel

QUICK TEST

1. What is the main use of iron?
2. What must be present for iron to rust?
3. How does oiling an iron object stop it from rusting?
4. Name a metal that could be used in sacrificial protection to stop iron rusting.
5. Give four properties of cast iron.
6. What is the main impurity in cast iron?
7. What is the name given to very pure iron?
8. Why is pure iron soft?
9. Which non-metal element is used to make steel?
10. Which metals can be alloyed to form stainless steel?

IRON AND STEEL · Chemistry

Aluminium

Aluminium is abundant in the Earth's crust, but it is also very reactive. Consequently, aluminium is more expensive than iron.

Bauxite

The main ore of aluminium is called **bauxite**; it contains the compound aluminium oxide, Al_2O_3. Unfortunately, bauxite is often found in environmentally sensitive areas such as the Amazonian rainforests. Extracting bauxite from these places brings jobs and money to the area. However, it can also scar the landscape and damage resident wildlife. New roads may damage the areas around the mines and result in local people being displaced.

Recycling aluminium

One way to protect the areas where bauxite is found is simply for people to **recycle** their old aluminium cans. **Recycling** has many advantages:
- We will not have to extract so much bauxite.
- Landfill sites will not be filled up with discarded aluminium cans.
- It uses much less energy than extracting aluminium straight from its ore.

Properties of aluminium

Although pure aluminium is quite soft, it becomes much stronger when it is alloyed with other metals. **Aluminium alloys combine high strength with low density.** This makes aluminium a very useful metal for making objects like aeroplanes and mountain bikes.

Aluminium is quite a reactive metal and yet it is widely used to make drinks cans. In fact, aluminium appears to be much less reactive than its position in the reactivity series suggests. This is because when aluminium objects are made, their surfaces quickly react with oxygen to form a thin **layer of aluminium oxide**. This layer stops the aluminium metal from coming into contact with other chemicals and so prevents any further reaction. It also means that it is quite safe for us to drink fizzy, acidic drinks from aluminium cans.

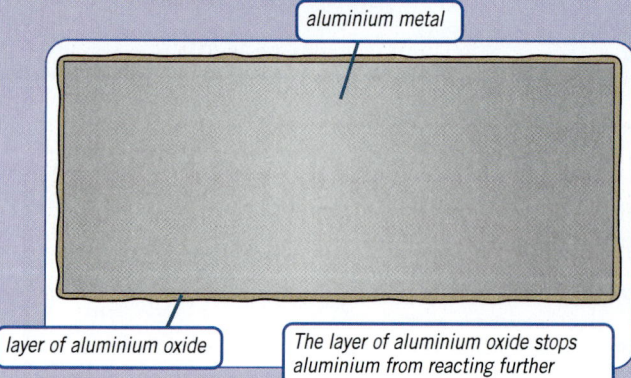

The layer of aluminium oxide stops aluminium from reacting further

The extraction of aluminium

Aluminium is more reactive than carbon so it is extracted using electrolysis, even though this is a very expensive method. The main ore of aluminium, bauxite, contains aluminium oxide. For electrolysis to occur, the aluminium ions and oxide ions in bauxite must be able to move. This means that the bauxite has to be either heated until it melts or dissolved in something.

Bauxite has a very high melting point and heating the ore to this temperature would be very expensive. Fortunately, another ore of aluminium called **cryolite** has a much lower melting point. First the cryolite is heated until it melts and then the bauxite is **dissolved** in the molten cryolite.

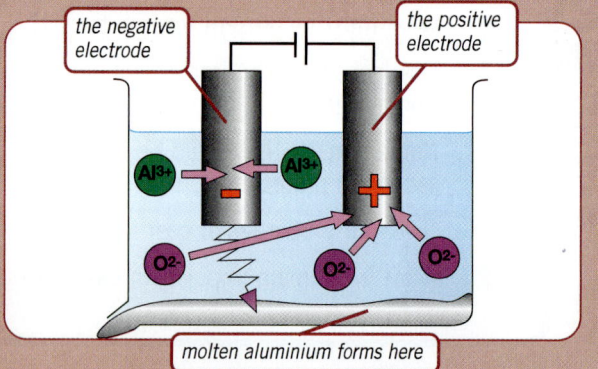

Electrolysis

Aluminium can now be extracted by electrolysis.

1 By dissolving the aluminium oxide, both the aluminium Al^{3+} and the oxide O^{2-} ions can move.

2 During electrolysis the Al^{3+} ions are attracted to the negative electrode where they pick up electrons to form Al atoms. The aluminium metal accumulates at the bottom of the cell where it can be collected.

aluminium ions	+	electrons	→	aluminium atoms
Al^{3+}	+	$3e^-$	→	Al

3 The O^{2-} ions are attracted to the positive electrode where they deposit electrons to form oxygen molecules.

oxide ions	−	electrons	→	oxygen molecules
$2O^{2-}$	−	$4e^-$	→	O_2

4 The oxygen that forms at the positive electrode readily reacts with the **carbon, graphite electrode** to form carbon dioxide. The electrodes, therefore, must be replaced periodically.

Oxidation and reduction

In the electrolysis of aluminium oxide:

- **Aluminium ions are reduced to aluminium atoms.**
- **Oxide ions are oxidised to oxygen molecules.**

Reduction reactions occur when a species gains electrons. Here, each aluminium ion gains three electrons to form an aluminium atom.

Oxidation reactions occur when a species loses electrons. Here, two oxide ions both lose two electrons to form an oxygen molecule.

Reduction and oxidation reactions must always occur together and so are sometimes referred to as **redox** reactions.

> *Oxidation and reduction can be remembered using 'OIL RIG'. Oxidation Is Loss Reduction Is Gain (of electrons).*

Aluminium drinks cans

KEY TERMS

Make sure you understand these terms before moving on!
- bauxite
- recycling
- density
- extraction
- cryolite
- reduction
- oxidation

QUICK TEST

1. Name the main ore of aluminium.
2. Give two properties of pure aluminium.
3. What is a mixture of metals called?
4. Why is aluminium less reactive than expected?
5. What is the formula of aluminium oxide?
6. What is the name of the method used to extract aluminium from its ore?
7. During the electrolysis of aluminium oxide which ions are oxidised?
8. During the electrolysis of aluminium oxide which ions are reduced?
9. What are the electrodes made from?
10. Why should the electrodes be periodically replaced?

Titanium and copper

Despite being abundant in the Earth's crust, titanium is an expensive metal.

Properties of titanium

Titanium has some very special properties:

- It is very strong when alloyed with other metals.
- It has a very low density.
- It has a very high melting point.
- It is very resistant to corrosion.

Titanium appears to be unreactive because the surface of titanium objects quickly reacts with oxygen to form a **layer of titanium oxide**.

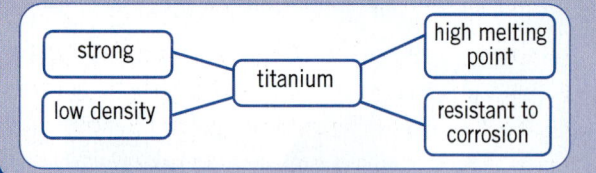

Uses of titanium

Titanium's properties make it a very useful metal. Titanium **alloys** are used to make:

- replacement hip and elbow joints
- aircraft

This F22 fighter is made from a titanium alloy

Titanium ore

The main **ore** of titanium is rutile. Rutile contains the compound **titanium dioxide** TiO_2. Rutile is a very hard mineral that is resistant to weathering and is found mixed amongst sand on certain beaches.

Extraction of titanium

Titanium is more reactive than carbon and so it cannot be extracted simply by heating titanium dioxide with carbon. The **extraction** of titanium is quite a complicated process.

- First, the titanium dioxide is converted to **titanium chloride**.
- Then the titanium chloride is reacted with **molten magnesium**. Magnesium is more reactive than titanium and a chemical reaction takes place in which titanium is displaced.

titanium chloride	+	magnesium	→	titanium	+	magnesium chloride
$TiCl_4$	+	$2Mg$	→	Ti	+	$2MgCl_2$

This reaction is carried out in a vacuum to stop the titanium from reacting with oxygen in the air to form titanium dioxide.

Smart alloys

Smart alloys are new materials with amazing properties. They have one or more properties that can be dramatically altered by changes in the environment.

One famous example of a smart alloy is **nitinol**. Nitinol is an alloy of nickel and titanium that has a shape memory. When a force is applied to a smart alloy it is stretched. However, when a smart alloy is then heated up it returns to its original shape.

Copper

Copper is an unreactive metal that has been known since ancient times.

Copper has some very special properties:

- It is a good **thermal conductor**.
- It is a good electrical conductor.
- It is easy to shape.
- It is very unreactive.

Uses of copper

Copper's properties mean that it is a very useful metal. Copper is used to make:

- water pipes
- saucepans
- electrical wires.

This saucepan is made from copper. Copper is a good thermal conductor and does not contaminate the food that is being cooked

Purification of copper

Copper must be purified before it can be used for certain applications such as in high specification wiring. Copper is purified using **electrolysis**.

> *Electrolysis involves passing an electrical current through a molten ionic substance or dissolving an ionic substance to break down the substance into simpler parts.*

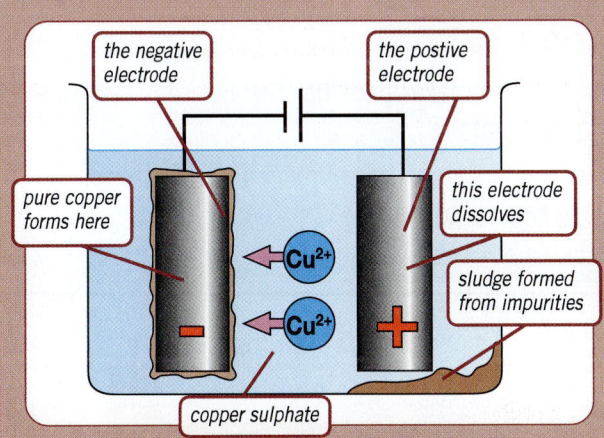

Labels on diagram: the negative electrode; the positive electrode; pure copper forms here; this electrode dissolves; sludge formed from impurities; Cu^{2+}; copper sulphate

- During the electrolysis of copper, the impure copper metal is used as the positive electrode.
- At the positive electrode, the copper atoms give up electrons to form copper ions.

$$\text{copper atoms} - \text{electrons} \rightarrow \text{copper ions}$$
$$Cu - 2e^- \rightarrow Cu^{2+}$$

- As the positive electrode dissolves away, any impurities fall to the bottom of the cell to form sludge.
- Copper ions in the solution are attracted towards the negative electrode.
- At the negative electrode, the copper ions gain electrons to form copper atoms.

$$\text{Copper ions} + \text{electrons} \rightarrow \text{copper atoms}$$
$$Cu^{2+} + 2e^- \rightarrow Cu$$

Overall, the positive electrode gets smaller while the negative electrode gets bigger. In addition, the negative electrode is covered in very pure copper.

Copper ore

Copper has several ores. However, as copper has been known for such a long time, the richest ores have now been exhausted. Today we use copper ores which can easily be converted into copper oxide. Copper can be extracted from copper oxide by removing the oxygen. This is called reduction.

Copper can be extracted from its ore, chalcopyrite

Copper alloys

Pure copper is too soft for many uses. In pure copper, the atoms are all the same size and so they form a regular arrangement. Copper is soft because the layers of atoms can pass easily over each other.

Copper is often mixed with other metals to form alloys. **Bronze is made by mixing copper and tin. Brass is made by mixing copper and zinc.**

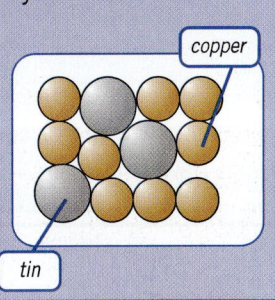

Labels: copper; tin

KEY TERMS
- alloy
- ore
- extraction
- thermal conductor
- electrolysis

QUICK TEST

1. How can titanium be made stronger?
2. Why does titanium appear to be unreactive?
3. How is titanium used inside the human body?
4. What is the main ore of titanium?
5. What is the chemical name of the main ore of titanium?
6. Give the symbol equation for the reaction that takes place at the negative electrode during the purification of copper.

Transition metals

Metals have a *giant structure*. In metals, the electrons in the highest energy shells (the outer electrons) are not bound to one atom, but are free to move through the whole structure. This means that metals consist of positive metals ions surrounded by a sea of negative electrons. *Metallic bonding is the attraction between these ions and the electrons.*

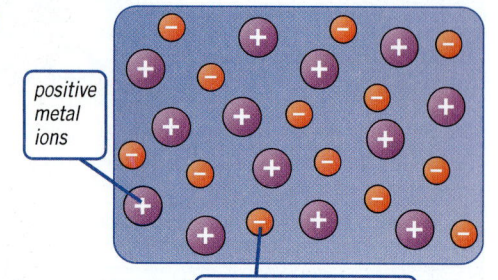

Properties of metals

Metallic bonding means that metals have several very useful properties:

- The free electrons mean that metals are **good electrical conductors**.
- The free electrons also mean that metals are **good thermal conductors**.
- The strong attraction between the metal ions and the electrons means that metals can be drawn into **wires** as the ions slide over each other.
- Metals can also be **hammered into shape**.

The transition metals are found in the middle section of the **periodic table**. Copper, iron and nickel are examples of very useful transition metals. All transition metals have characteristic properties. They have:

- a **high melting point** (except for mercury which is a liquid at room temperature)
- a **high density**
- coloured compounds

They are also strong, tough and hard wearing. All transition metals are much less reactive than Group 1 metals. They all react less vigorously with oxygen and water.

Many transition metals can **form ions with different charges**. This makes transition metals useful catalysts in many reactions.

Transition metals all have similar properties because they have similar electron structures.

Copper

- Copper is a good electrical and thermal conductor.
- It can be easily bent into new shapes and does not corrode.
- Copper is widely used in electrical wiring.
- It is also used to make water pipes.

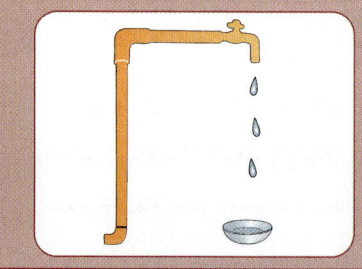

Iron

- Iron made in the blast furnace is strong but brittle.
- Iron is often made into steel.
- Steel is strong and cheap and is used in vast quantities. However, it is also heavy and may rust.
- Iron and steel are useful structural materials. They are used to make buildings, bridges, ships, cars and trains.
- Iron is used as a catalyst in the Haber process.

Gold

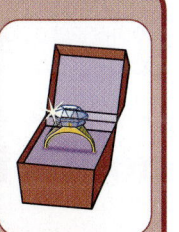

- Gold is rare and this makes it valuable.
- Gold is shiny and unreactive but too soft for many uses.
- Gold can be mixed with other metals.
- It is widely used to make jewellery.

Nickel

- Nickel is hard, shiny and dense.
- It is widely used to make coins.
- Nickel is used as a catalyst in the manufacture of margarine.

Silver

- Silver is shiny and quite unreactive.
- It has the highest electrical and thermal conductivity of any metal.
- It is used to make coins, jewellery and cutlery.

Metal alloys

Alloys are made by mixing metals together. In fact, mixing metals with non-metals can occasionally make alloys.

Common alloys include:

- Amalgams, which are mainly mercury.
- Brass, which is made from copper and zinc.
- Bronze, which is made from copper and tin.
- Solder, which is made from lead and tin.
- Steel, which is mainly iron.

KEY TERMS

Make sure you understand these terms before moving on!
- giant structure
- electrical conductors
- thermal conductors
- periodic table
- density
- alloys

TRANSITION METALS — Chemistry

QUICK TEST

1. Why are metals able to conduct heat and electricity?
2. In which part of the periodic table are the transition metals found?
3. What are the characteristics of transition metals?
4. Why is copper used for electrical wiring?
5. Why is copper used for water pipes?
6. Why is iron made into steel?
7. Which items can be made from steel?
8. In which process is iron used as a catalyst?
9. Which items can be made from nickel?
10. Nickel is used as a catalyst for the manufacture of which foodstuff?

The noble gases

The noble gases are very unreactive. They are sometimes described as being '*inert*' because they do not react. This is because they have a full, *stable*, outer shell of electrons.

A model showing the outer shell of electrons

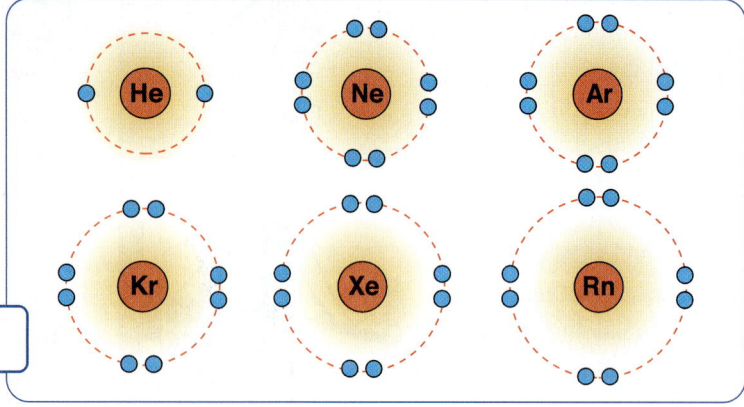

Characteristics of noble gases

- The noble gases are found on the far right-hand side of the periodic table.
- The noble gases are all colourless.
- They are monatomic gases. This means that they exist as single atoms rather than as diatomic molecules as other gases do.

Why do melting and boiling points increase down the group?

- Melting and boiling points increase down the group because the atoms get larger and have more electrons.
- This means that the strength of the attraction between atoms increases.
- The **forces of attraction between atoms get stronger** down the group, and so it takes more energy to overcome these forces. As a consequence, noble gases will melt and boil at increasingly higher temperatures.

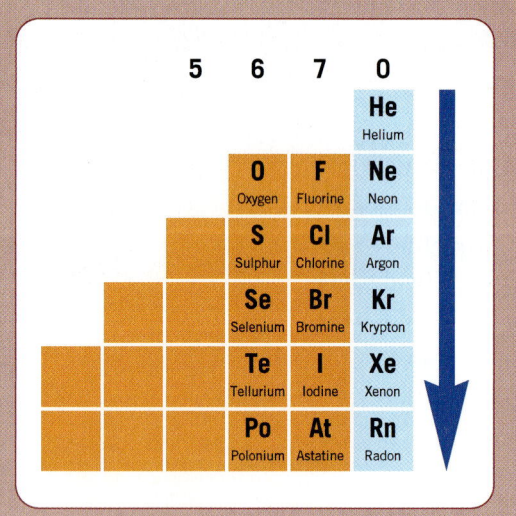

Why are noble gases so unreactive?

When atoms react, they share, gain or lose electrons in order to obtain a full outer shell of electrons. **Noble gases already have a full and stable outer shell so they do not react**. Noble gases are useful precisely because they do not react.

Uses of noble gases

Helium
- Helium is used in balloons and in airships.
- It is less dense than air.
- It is not **flammable**. (Early airships used hydrogen, which is flammable and this caused problems.)

Neon
- Neon is used in electrical discharge tubes in advertising signs.

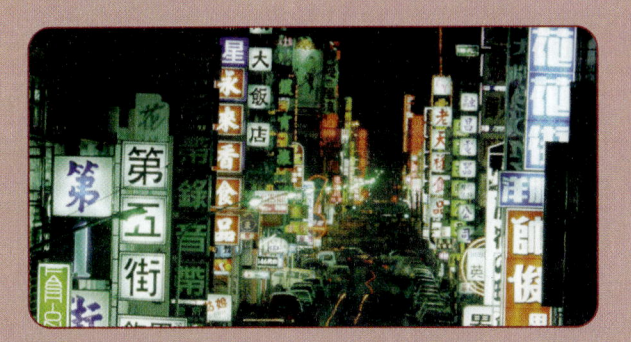

Argon
- Argon is used in filament light bulbs.
- Surrounding the hot filament with argon stops the filament from burning away and breaking the bulb.

Krypton
- Krypton is used in lasers.

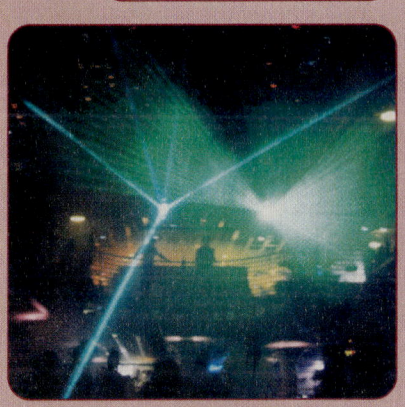

Radon
- Radon is a noble gas. It is chemically unreactive but it is radioactive. Home owners in some parts of the country such as Cornwall and Northamptonshire use these devices to monitor radon levels.

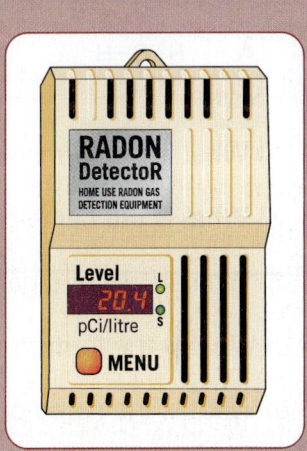

KEY TERMS

Make sure you understand these terms before moving on!
- inert
- stable
- periodic table
- monatomic
- flammable

QUICK TEST

1. Why are the noble gases so unreactive?
2. What is the trend in boiling point down the group?
3. Draw the (outer shell) electron shell of helium.
4. Draw the (outer shell) electron shell of argon.
5. What does 'monatomic' mean?
6. What is helium used for?
7. Why is it used?
8. What is neon used for?
9. What is argon used for?
10. What is krypton used for?

Practice questions

Use the questions to test your progress. Check your answers on page 111.

1. This table is about limestone and some of the substances that can be made from limestone.

Substance	Information about the substance
A	is made when limestone is heated with silica and soda
B	is made when water is added to calcium oxide
C	is a rock that contains large amounts of calcium carbonate
D	is formed when calcium carbonate is heated

   a) What is the name of substance C? ....

   b) What is the chemical formula of substance D? ....

   c) What is the name of substance B? ....

   d) What is the name of substance A? ....

2. Atoms can join together to form molecules. Here are four diagrams of molecules.

   A: $H-CH_2-H$ (with H above and below central C)
   B: $H-CH_2-CH_2-H$ (ethane structural)
   C: $H_2C=CH_2$ (ethene structural)
   D: $H-CH_2-CH=CH_2$ (propene structural)

   a) What is the formula of molecule A? ....

   b) What is the name of molecule B? ....

   c) What family of organic compounds do molecules A and B belong to? ....

   d) What is the formula of molecule C? ....

   e) What is the name of molecule D? ....

   f) What family of organic compounds do molecules C and D belong to? ....

3. Crude oil can be separated into fractions.

   a) What is the name of the process used to separate crude oil into fractions? ....

   b) Molecules found in the diesel oil fraction contain about twenty carbon atoms. Molecules in the petrol fraction have about eight carbon atoms. Tick one box to show how petrol and diesel molecules compare.
   Compared with diesel molecules, petrol molecules are:
   ☐ more flammable
   ☐ more viscous
   ☐ have a higher boiling point
   ☐ have more carbon atoms

   c) Some long hydrocarbon molecules can be split into smaller, more useful molecules. What is the name of the process used to break up long hydrocarbon molecules into shorter more useful hydrocarbons?

   ....

4. Which of these diagrams represents a molecule of butane, C_4H_{10}?

A
$$\begin{array}{ccc} H & H & H \\ | & | & | \\ H-C-C-C-H \\ | & | & | \\ H & H & H \end{array}$$

B
$$\begin{array}{cccc} H & H & H & H \\ | & | & | & | \\ H-C-C-C-C-H \\ | & | & | & | \\ H & H & H & H \end{array}$$

C
$$\begin{array}{cccc} H & H & H & H \\ & | & | & | \\ C=C-C-C-H \\ | & & | & | \\ H & & H & H \end{array}$$

D
$$\begin{array}{cccc} & & & H \\ & & & | \\ H & H-C-H \\ | & | \\ H-C-C=C \\ | & | & | \\ H & H & H \end{array}$$

....

5. a) What is the name given to a mixture of metals? ....

b) Which non-metal element is often added to steel to make it harder? ....

6. Here is a sketch of the atoms in pure titanium.

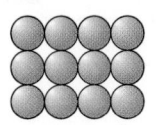

Here is a sketch of the atoms in a titanium alloy.

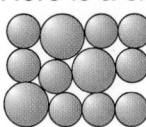

Explain why a titanium alloy is stronger than pure titanium.

7. Iron is produced in the blast furnace. Place these statements in order to show how iron is produced.

A) Carbon dioxide reacts with carbon to form carbon monoxide

B) The iron is dense and sinks to the bottom of the furnace where it can be removed.

C) Carbon reacts with oxygen to form carbon dioxide.

D) The carbon monoxide reacts with iron oxide to form iron and carbon dioxide.

....

8. This table shows the names of four different metals.

Name of metal
aluminium
iron
copper
gold

a) Which of these metals is more reactive than carbon? ....

b) Which of these metals is extracted from its ore bauxite? ....

c) Which metal can be alloyed to form steel? ....

d) Which of these metals is the least reactive? ....

Energy

Energy is one of the most talked about and written about issues of our times. In our everyday lives, we take it for granted that when we need energy to warm our buildings, cook our food, help us communicate with each other, to travel and so on, it will be there. In the future, however, this may all change. Our *sources of energy* may become *depleted*. A second equally important problem is that our demand and use of energy may be causing irreversible changes to our climate. It is important that we look at these problems now and begin to find solutions before it is too late.

Cities like this need large amounts of energy

Types of energy

First, let's remind ourselves of the different forms of energy:

Types of energy	Sources
heat or thermal energy	hot objects, such as fires
light energy	the Sun, light bulbs, lamps, etc.
sound energy	loudspeakers, vibrating objects
electrical energy	this is carried around a circuit whenever a current flows
chemical energy	food, fuels and batteries
kinetic energy (the energy an object has because it is moving)	flowing water, wind, etc.
elastic or strain potential energy	objects such as springs and rubber bands that are stretched or twisted e.g. clockwork radio
gravitational potential energy	objects that have a high position and are able to fall e.g. water at the top of a waterfall
nuclear energy	reactions in the centre or nucleus of an atom

chemical energy in the wax

elastic potential energy in the rubber

gravitational potential energy in the water at the top of the waterfall

chemical energy in the battery

Energy transfer

When we use energy to do something for us **it does not disappear**. Energy cannot be created or destroyed. It is just **transferred into other forms** of energy.

electrical energy → light energy / heat energy

A **light bulb** transfers **electrical energy** into **heat and light energy**.

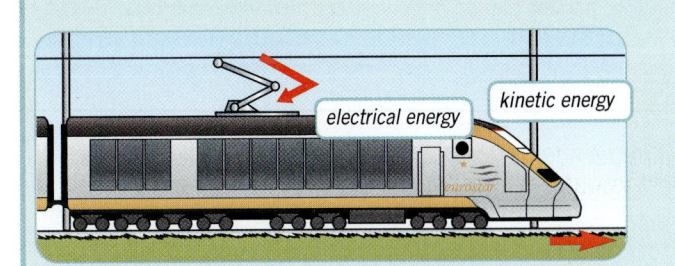

electrical energy → sound energy

A **loudspeaker** transfers **electrical energy** into **sound energy**.

electrical energy → kinetic energy

The **motor** inside this locomotive transfers **electrical energy** into **kinetic energy**.

When this **lift** travels upwards, **electrical energy** is being transferred into **gravitational potential energy**.

Here are some other examples of energy transfers:

Energy in	Energy changer	Energy out
electrical	television	light, sound and heat
electrical	battery charger	chemical
electrical	electric fire	heat and light
chemical	firework	heat, light and sound
light	solar cell	electrical
kinetic	wind turbine	electrical
chemical	battery	electrical
strain potential energy	clockwork car	kinetic
sound	microphone	electrical
kinetic energy	generator	electrical

We often use **electrical devices** because they will transfer energy at the flick of a switch. It is also easy to move electrical energy over large distances using wires and cables.

KEY TERMS

Make sure you understand these terms before moving on!
- sources of energy
- depleted
- energy transfer
- electrical devices

QUICK TEST

1. Name five different types of energy.
2. Name two types of energy which can be stored.
3. Name three devices that transfer electrical energy.
4. What kind of energy does a crate gain as it is lifted by an electric hoist?
5. Can you think of an electrical appliance in your house which changes electrical energy into heat, sound and kinetic energy?
6. Why is electrical energy a very convenient form of energy?
7. Give one example of where electrical energy is moved a distance of about a) 1 m, b) 10–20 m and c) more than 1 km.

Efficiency

Many devices take in one form of energy and transform it into another. It is important that we know how efficiently they do this so that we can choose between them and, where possible, try to improve them.

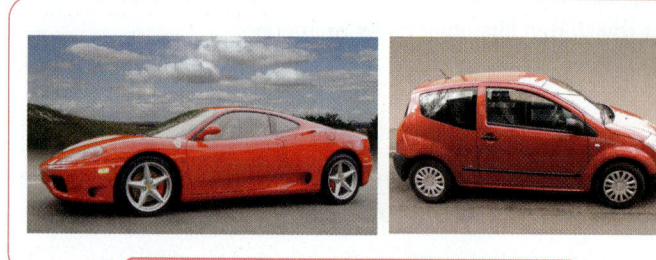

Most of us, given the choice, would probably choose the car on the left, but is it the most efficient machine, or just a 'gas guzzler' that wastes energy?

Efficiency

Usually when an energy transfer takes place, only part of the energy is transformed into something useful. The remainder is **wasted**. The table below contains some examples.

Energy input	Device	Useful energy output	Wasted energy
electrical	television	light and sound	heat
chemical	car	kinetic energy	heat and sound
electrical	electric motor	kinetic energy	heat and sound
chemical	candle	light	heat

This wasted energy is eventually transferred to the **surroundings**, which become warmer. The greater the percentage of energy that is usefully transformed by a device, the more efficient the device is.

Seeing the light 1

A vast amount of energy is used to produce light at night-time, particularly in large towns and cities. However, are the devices we use efficient?

The bulb to the right is not 100% efficient. Only a part of the electrical energy is transferred into light. Some of it is transferred into heat. To calculate the efficiency of a transfer we use the equation:

$$\text{Efficiency} = \frac{\text{useful energy transferred by the device}}{\text{total energy supplied to the device}} \times 100\%$$

In this case, 200 J of electrical energy enter the bulb, of which 8 J is transferred into light energy and 192 J is transferred into heat.

$$\text{Efficiency} = \frac{\text{useful energy transferred by the device}}{\text{total energy supplied to the device}} \times 100\%$$

$$\text{The efficiency of the bulb} = \frac{8\ J}{200\ J} \times 100\% = 4\%.$$

This is a very **inefficient energy transfer** and yet we use so many of them. Are there any alternatives?

Seeing the light 2

What about strip lights?

$$\text{Efficiency} = \frac{\text{useful energy transferred by the device}}{\text{total energy supplied to the device}} \times 100\%$$

The efficiency of the fluorescent light = $\frac{30 \text{ J}}{200 \text{ J}} \times 100\% = 15\%$.

We can see from these figures that a fluorescent light is much more efficient than a traditional light bulb. Nevertheless, it is still not very good and lots of work is being done to try and find better replacements. One example which is now available in shops is the **compact fluorescent bulb** shown to the right.

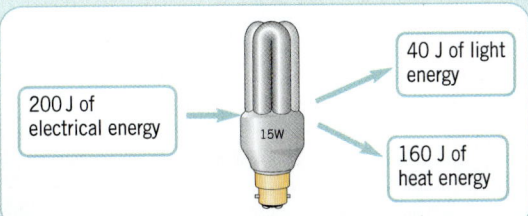

$$\text{Efficiency} = \frac{\text{useful energy transferred by the device}}{\text{total energy supplied to the device}} \times 100\%$$

The efficiency of the compact fluorescent light = $\frac{40 \text{ J}}{200 \text{ J}} \times 100\% = 20\%$.

An efficient device saves money and helps protect the environment by reducing energy consumption. An inefficient device wastes energy and helps deplete energy resources.

KEY TERMS

Make sure you understand these terms before moving on!
- efficiency
- wasted
- surroundings
- inefficient energy transfer

QUICK TEST

1. Suggest an energy transfer which might be taking place with a CD player that will make it less than 100% efficient.
2. Calculate the efficiency of a radio that changes 200 J of electrical energy into 180 J of sound energy.
3. Calculate the efficiency of a battery charger which changes 500 J of electrical energy into 350 J of chemical energy. The remaining 150 J of energy is transferred into non-useful forms.
4. Calculate the efficiency of a television which changes 300 J of electrical energy into 100 J of light and sound energy. The remaining 200 J of energy is transferred into non-useful forms.
5. Calculate the efficiency of a radio which changes just 15 J of electrical energy into sound. The remaining 35 J of electrical energy is transferred to the surroundings as heat.
6. If a bulb is 5% efficient, how much energy is wasted when it transfers 400 J of electrical energy?
7. Why is it important for scientists to develop more efficient devices?

Generating electricity

Electricity is one of the most convenient forms of energy. It is easily converted into other forms of energy and it can be transferred across large distances.

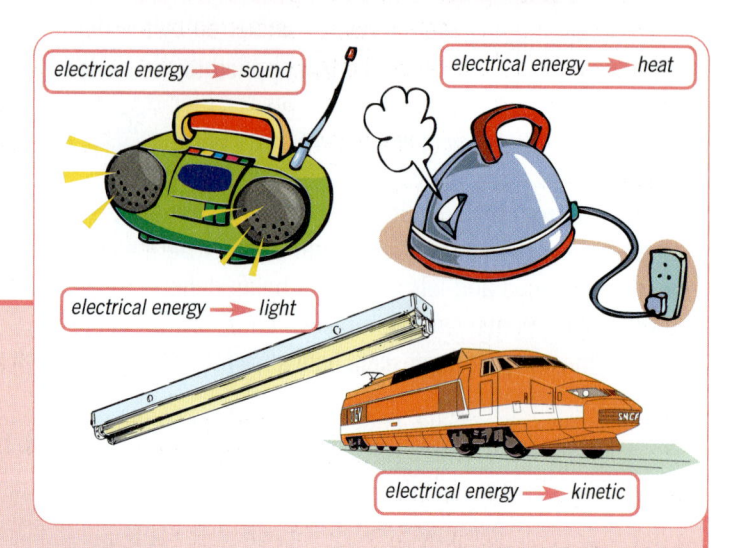

electrical energy → sound
electrical energy → heat
electrical energy → light
electrical energy → kinetic

Power stations

Most of the electrical energy we use at home is generated at **power stations**. There are several different types of power station including those that use coal, **oil or gas as their source of energy** (**fuel**).

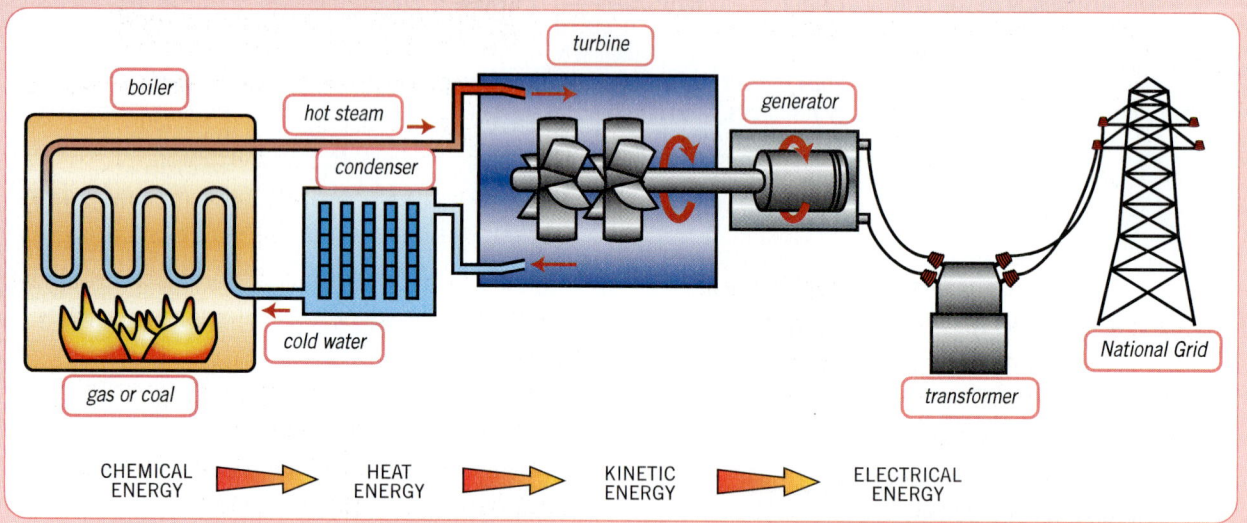

CHEMICAL ENERGY → HEAT ENERGY → KINETIC ENERGY → ELECTRICAL ENERGY

- The fuel is burned to release its **chemical energy**.
- The **heat energy released** is used to heat water and turn it into **steam**.
- The steam **turns turbines**.
- The turbines **turn large generators**.
- The **generators produce electrical energy**.
- The electrical energy is carried to our homes through the National Grid.

Before entering the National Grid, the electrical energy passes through step-up transformers which increase its voltage and decrease the current. These changes reduce the energy losses in the cables and wires. When the electrical energy is close to its final destination it again passes through transformers, but this time they are step-down transformers. They decrease the voltage to much safer levels, e.g. 230 V.

Fossil fuels

Coal, oil and gas are called **fossil fuels**. They are **concentrated sources** of energy.

Fossil fuels are formed from **plants and animals** that died over 100 million years ago.

Having died, they were **covered with many layers of mud and earth**. The resulting **large pressures and high temperatures** changed them into fossil fuels. Since they take **millions of years to form**, these fuels are called **non-renewable sources of energy**. Once they have been used up they **cannot be replaced**.

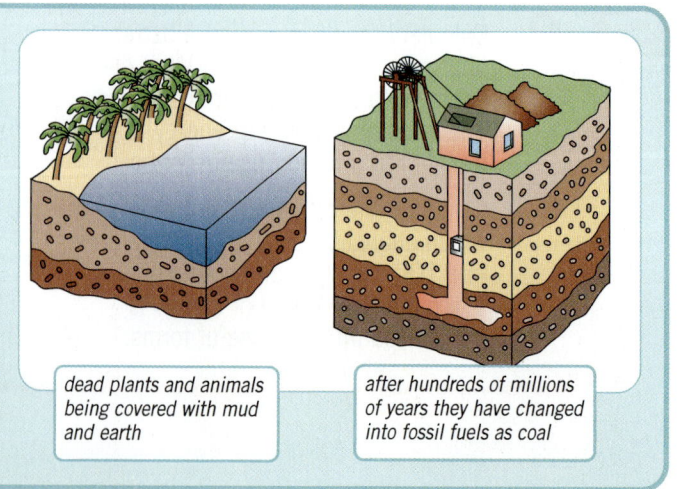

dead plants and animals being covered with mud and earth

after hundreds of millions of years they have changed into fossil fuels as coal

The problems with fossil fuels

- When fossil fuels are burned they produce **carbon dioxide**. Increasing the amount of carbon dioxide in the atmosphere will cause the temperature of the Earth and its atmosphere to rise. **This is called the greenhouse effect and could lead to drastic changes in climate, flooding and drought.**
- When coal and oil are burned they produce gases that cause **acid rain**.
- **Environmental problems** are created by **mining** and **spillage of oil during transport**.
- We are using fossil fuels up very quickly and will soon have to find other sources of energy, but we need to start looking now.

The solutions

We need to slow down the rate at which we are using fossil fuels so that they will last longer. There are several ways we can do this:

- **Reduce petrol consumption** by driving smaller cars, using public transport or walking or cycling. We should also develop more efficient car engines.
- **Improve the insulation** to our homes and factories so less energy is wasted heating them.
- **Increase public awareness** of how they are wasting energy so that they turn off lights and turn down heating where possible.
- We need to use other sources of energy. **Renewable sources of energy** such as wind, waves, tidal, solar, geothermal, biomass and hydroelectric **need to be developed**. Each of these sources has some advantages and disadvantages.

In the UK, some of our electricity is generated by nuclear power stations.

Here uranium or plutonium (the fuel) undergoes a kind of nuclear reaction called fission which releases large amounts of energy. This energy is used to heat water, creating the steam needed to drive the turbines.

These power stations have the advantage of producing electrical energy without emitting greenhouse or other **polluting gases** and the actual cost of producing electricity is very low. There are, however, several very serious disadvantages which need to be considered:

- The building and **decommissioning** (taking out of use and demolishing) of nuclear power stations is very expensive.
- **Nuclear waste** material will remain dangerously radioactive for thousands of years.
- There is always the possibility of leaks into the atmosphere of radioactive materials.
- There is the risk of a nuclear explosion.

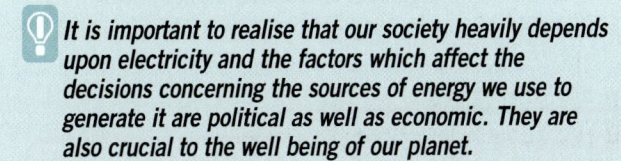

> *It is important to realise that our society heavily depends upon electricity and the factors which affect the decisions concerning the sources of energy we use to generate it are political as well as economic. They are also crucial to the well being of our planet.*

KEY TERMS

Make sure you understand these terms before moving on!
- turbines
- generators
- National Grid
- fossil fuels
- non-renewable sources of energy
- greenhouse effect
- acid rain
- environmental problems
- polluting gases
- decommissioning
- nuclear waste

QUICK TEST

1. Name three fossil fuels.
2. Name a fuel which is used in some power stations but is not a fossil fuel.
3. What gas causes the greenhouse effect?
4. Which fossil fuels when burned cause acid rain?
5. Name one type of environmental damage that might be caused as a result of using fossil fuels in our power stations.
6. Why are fossil fuels called non-renewable sources of energy?
7. Suggest three ways in which we could make fossil fuels last longer.
8. Sweden generates most of its electricity using nuclear power stations. Give two reasons why Sweden has decided to do this even though it has fossil fuels.

Renewable sources of energy

Unlike fossil fuels, there are some sources of energy which will not run out. They are continually being replaced. These are called *renewable sources of energy*. Each of these sources has advantages and disadvantages to their use. *We need to consider all of these carefully before we make any choices.*

Wind power

The **kinetic energy of the wind** is used to drive turbines and generators.

+ It is a **renewable** source of energy and therefore will not be exhausted.
+ It has **low level technology** and therefore can be used by developing countries.
+ There is **no atmospheric pollution**.
− It creates **visual and noise pollution**.
− It is **limited to windy sites**.
− If there is **no wind, there is no energy**.

Hydroelectricity

The **kinetic energy of flowing water** is used to drive turbines and generators.

+ It is a **renewable source**.
+ Energy **can be stored** until required.
+ There is **no atmospheric pollution**.
− It involves **high initial cost**.
− It can mean a **high cost to the environment**, i.e. flooding, loss of habitat.

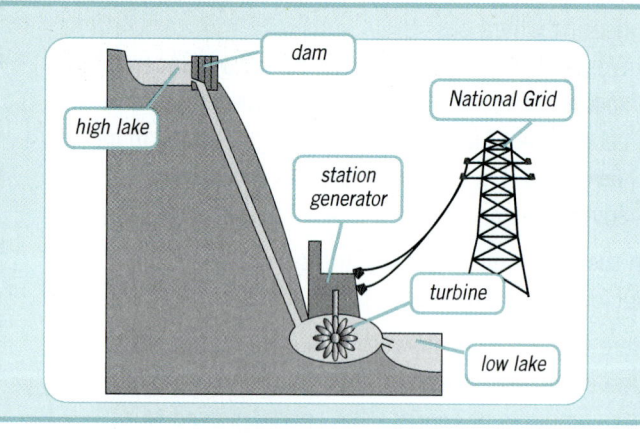

Wave power

The **rocking motion of the waves** is used to generate electricity.

+ It is a **renewable source**.
+ There is **no atmospheric pollution**.
+ It is **useful for isolated islands**.
− It involves **high initial cost**.
− It creates **visual pollution**.
− It has **poor energy capture**. A large area of machines is needed even for small energy return.

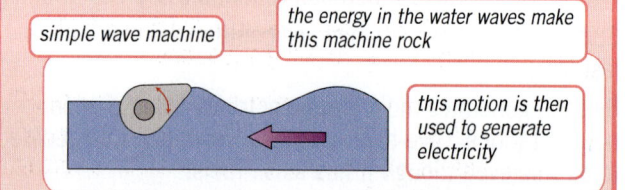

simple wave machine
the energy in the water waves make this machine rock
this motion is then used to generate electricity

Tidal power

At high tide, water is trapped behind a barrage or dam. At low tide, when it is released, the **gravitational potential energy of the water** changes into kinetic energy which then drives turbines and generates electricity.

+ It is a **renewable source**.
+ It is **reliable** – always two tides per day.
+ There is **no atmospheric pollution**.
+ It has **low running costs**.
− It involves **high initial cost**.
− It can mean **potential damage to environment**, e.g. flooding.
− It can be an **obstacle to water transport**.

Geothermal

In regions where the Earth's crust is thin, **hot rocks beneath the ground** can be used to heat water, turning it into steam. This steam is then used to drive turbines and generate electricity.

+ It is a **renewable source of energy**.
+ There is **no pollution and no environmental problems**.
− There are **very few suitable sites**.
− It involves a **high cost of drilling** deep into the ground.

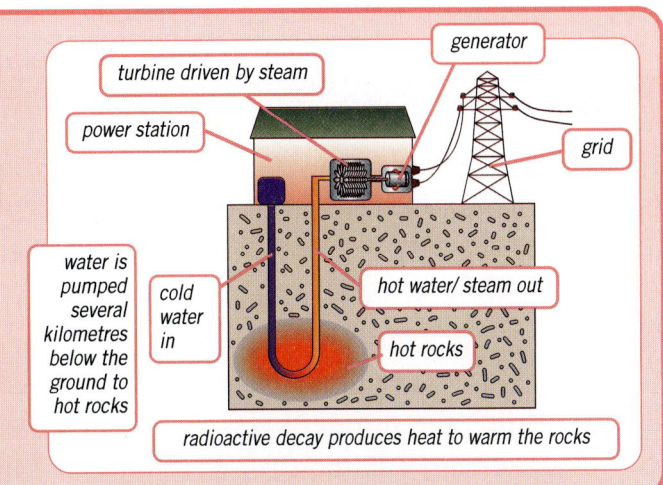

Diagram labels: generator; turbine driven by steam; power station; grid; water is pumped several kilometres below the ground to hot rocks; cold water in; hot water/steam out; hot rocks; radioactive decay produces heat to warm the rocks

Solar energy

The energy carried in the Sun's rays can be converted directly into electricity using solar cells.

Or the energy carried in the Sun's rays can be absorbed by dark coloured panels and used to heat water.

+ It is low maintenance.
+ There is no pollution from burning fuel.
+ There is no need for power cables.
− Initially it could be quite expensive.
− It may not be so useful in regions where there is limited sunshine.

This car uses no fuel at all. It transfers light energy from the Sun into electrical energy. This in turn is transferred into kinetic energy by its electric motor

Biomass

The **chemical energy stored in 'things that have grown'**, e.g. wood, can be **released by burning** them in a power station. This energy source can be maintained by growing a succession of trees and then cropping them when they mature.

+ It is a **renewable source of energy**.
+ It involves **low level technology** and therefore is useful in developing countries.
+ It does not add to the greenhouse effect as the carbon dioxide released when the things are burned was originally taken from the atmosphere as they grew.
− **Large areas of land are needed** to grow sufficient numbers of trees.

KEY TERMS

- renewable sources of energy
- wind power
- low level technology
- hydroelectricity
- wave power
- tidal power
- geothermal
- solar energy
- biomass
- biofuel

QUICK TEST

1. Name two energy resources which could be easily used and maintained in developing countries.
2. Name two sources of energy which could drive turbines directly.
3. Which of these energy sources might you use in the following situations:
   a) In a country where there is a hot desert?
   b) In a country where there is a rainforest?
   c) In a country where there is some volcanic action?
   d) In a country which has a long coastline?

Heat transfer – conduction

Heat will try to flow when there is a *temperature difference* between two places. It will flow from the hotter to the cooler place. *The bigger the temperature difference, the greater the rate at which the heat will flow.*

Sometimes this is desirable and we want to encourage it. Sometimes it is not and we want to try and prevent it. By understanding the different ways in which heat is transferred we can take measures to improve or reduce its flow rate depending upon the situation. *Conduction, convection* and *radiation* are three ways in which heat can move.

Conduction is *the movement of heat by passing on vibration energy.*

Conduction through solids

After five or ten minutes the whole length of this metal rod is hot.

Heat has been transferred along the rod by conduction.

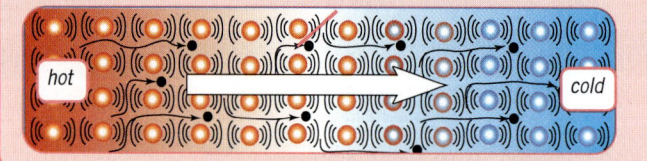

The atoms at the hot end **vibrate more violently as they gain energy** from the fire. **Free electrons collide with these atoms** and gain energy. The motions of these energetic electrons transfer energy to the cooler end of the rod.

All metals are good **conductors** of heat because:

- their atoms are **packed close together** and
- they have **large numbers of free electrons**.

Non-metals are usually poor conductors of heat because:

- their atoms are **further apart** and
- there are **no free electrons**.

An **insulator** is a material which **does not allow heat to travel through it easily**. Insulators are **used to prevent or reduce heat transfer.**

Heat transfer in the home 1

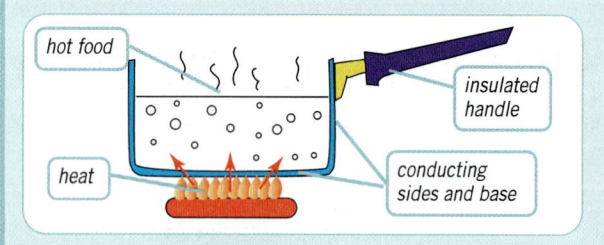

A good saucepan is made from materials that are **conductors** and **insulators**.

The base and sides of the pan are made of metal so that heat is easily conducted from the flame to the food. The handle is made from an insulator so that it does not become too hot to hold.

The particles in a gas are far apart. It is therefore very difficult for heat to pass through a gas by conduction. Gases are in fact excellent **insulators** and are often used in situations where we want to prevent the flow of heat.

It is impossible for heat to travel through a vacuum by conduction as it contains no particles.

Woven materials, e.g. wool and cotton, contain lots of **trapped air** and so are excellent **insulators**. This is why they keep you warm.

Heat transfer in the home 2

Glass fibre is an excellent insulator because it contains large amounts of **trapped air**. It is placed in the loft to reduce heat loss through the roof.

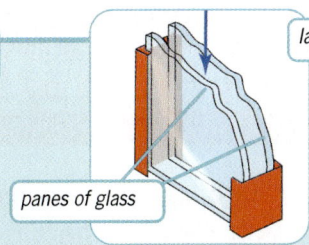

panes of glass — *layer of air*

Double glazing reduces heat loss from a house. It is the layer of air trapped between the two panes of glass that makes it difficult for the heat to escape

It is the layer of air trapped between the two panes of glass that make **double glazing** an excellent method of reducing heat loss from a house

Insulating the home

This diagram shows how heat may escape from a house that has not been insulated.

- *10% through windows, reduced by installing double glazing*
- *25% through roof, reduced by putting insulation into loft*
- *25% through walls, reduced by having cavity wall insulation*
- *25% through gaps and cracks around doors and windows, reduced by fitting draught excluders*
- *15% through floor, reduced by fitting carpets and underlay*

The cost of insulating a home

The table below shows the cost of the different types of insulation that can be used in the home and the annual savings that might result from each.

Type of insulation	Typical cost (£s)	Typical annual saving (£s)	Payback time (years)
double glazing	3000	50	60
cavity wall	500	100	5
loft insulation	250	125	2
draught excluders	100	20	5

> Make sure you understand the idea of **cost effectiveness**. A question about the cost effectiveness of different types of insulation is asking, 'How quickly will the savings pay for the extra insulation?' It is not asking which is the best insulator.

KEY TERMS

Make sure you understand these terms before moving on!
- temperature difference
- conduction
- conductors
- insulator
- double glazing
- cavity wall
- draught excluders
- cost effectiveness

QUICK TEST

1. Using the table below, work out the payback time and then a rank order for the cost effectiveness of the different methods of insulating your home.

Type of insulation	Typical cost (£s)	Typical annual saving (£s)	Payback time (years)	Rank order
double glazing	4000	100		
cavity wall	800	80		
loft insulation	210	70		
draught excluders	120	30		

HEAT TRANSFER – CONDUCTION

Physics

Heat transfer – convection

When the *burners are turned on, the air inside a balloon is warmed and expands*. As a result, it becomes less *dense* and rises, carrying its extra energy with it. If the *burners are turned off, the air cools and contracts*. It is now more dense and so begins to fall. This movement of air because of its expansion and contraction is called a *convection current* and can *transfer energy from place to place*.

Rising warm air will lift these balloons into the sky. But what will happen when the air cools?

Heating a room by convection

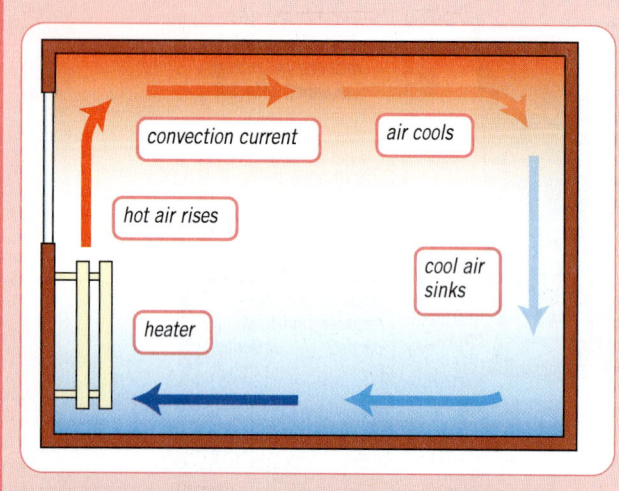

The energy is transferred to all parts of this room by convection. Note that the warmest air is next to the ceiling. The greatest loss of heat is likely to take place here unless there is insulation above the ceiling.

The traditional open fire we like to sit in front of is not very efficient at warming a room. It creates convection currents which transfer a lot of heat up the chimney and then it escapes to the surroundings. Modern gas fires and convector heaters are far more efficient.

Cavity walls

Many older homes have cavity walls which contain just air. Air is a good insulator and so reduces heat loss by conduction. However, heat can cross the gap if a convection current is set up.

To prevent this from happening we can inject foam insulation into the cavity. The foam contains lots of trapped air which is unable to move as part of a convection current.

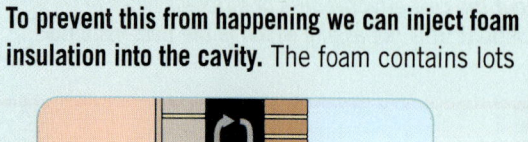

In modern houses, solid foam insulation boards are placed inside the cavity while the house is being built.

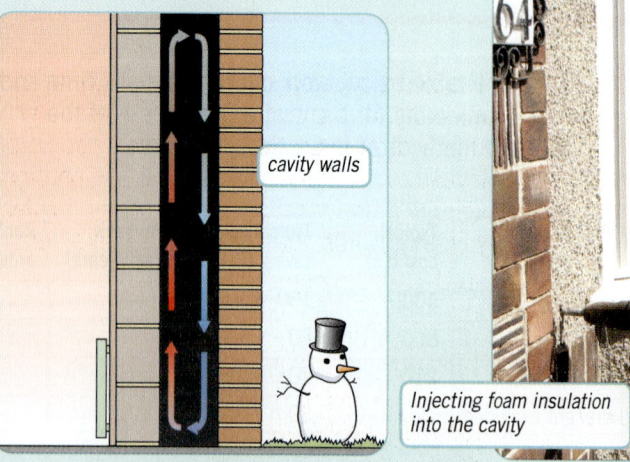

Injecting foam insulation into the cavity

Solid insulation boards placed between the two walls

86

Convection currents in ovens and fridges

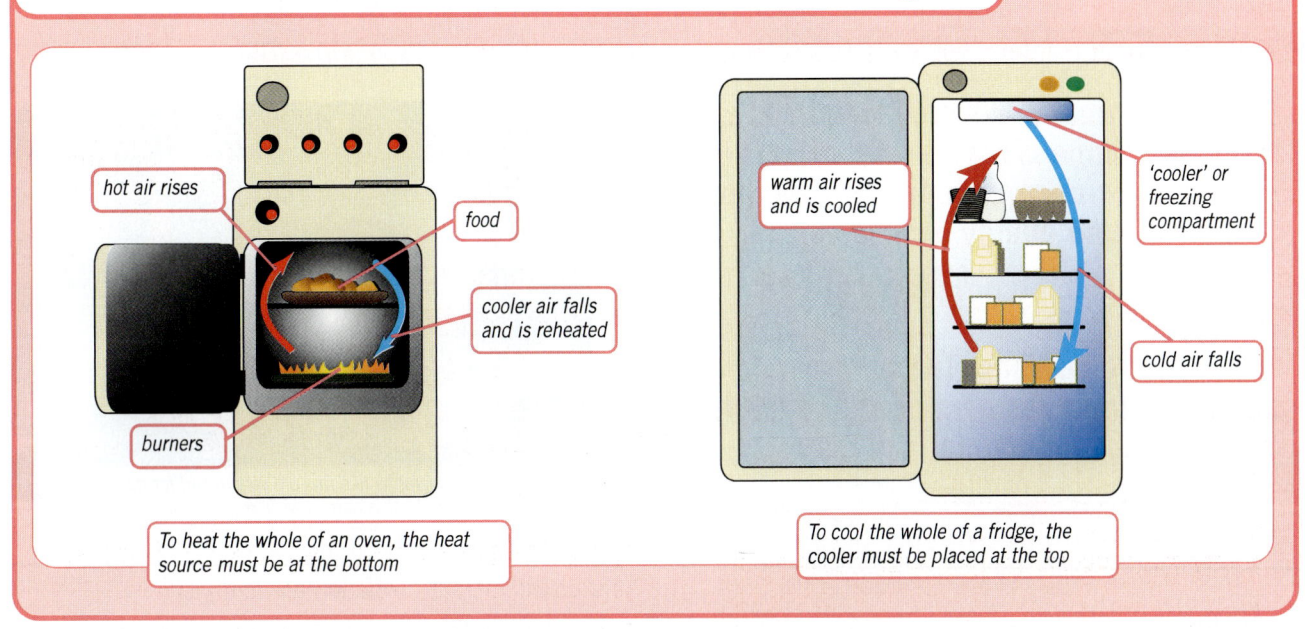

- hot air rises
- food
- cooler air falls and is reheated
- burners

To heat the whole of an oven, the heat source must be at the bottom

- warm air rises and is cooled
- 'cooler' or freezing compartment
- cold air falls

To cool the whole of a fridge, the cooler must be placed at the top

Sea breezes

Day — onshore breeze, hot land, cooler sea

During the daytime, the land is hotter than the sea and an onshore breeze is set up

Night — offshore breeze, cold land, warmer sea

During the night, the sea is warmer than the land and an offshore breeze is set up

It is a common mistake to say that heat rises. It is better to say that, when warmed, a gas becomes less dense and rises, taking heat energy with it.

KEY TERMS

Make sure you understand these terms before moving on!
- expands
- dense
- contracts
- convection current

HEAT TRANSFER — CONVECTION — Physics

QUICK TEST

1. Why does a gas rise when it is warmed?
2. What happens to a gas when it cools?
3. Why are traditional open fires inefficient?
4. Why should foam be placed inside a cavity wall?
5. Where should the freezing compartment of a fridge be placed so it cools the whole of a fridge?
6. In which direction will a sea breeze blow at midday during a hot summer?
7. The diagram below shows some simple mine workings. It is important the miners get a good supply of fresh air, but pumps have not yet been invented. The mine owners solve this problem by lighting a fire under one of the shafts. Explain in your own words how this solves the problem.

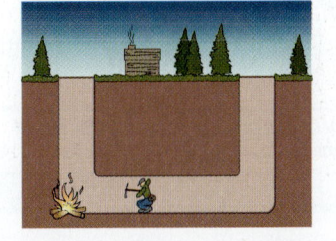

Heat transfer – radiation

All bodies *emit* and *absorb* thermal *radiation*. Thermal radiation is the transfer of heat by *electromagnetic waves* (infrared). The hotter a body, the more energy it *radiates*.

The photograph on the right is called a *thermogram*. It was taken using the radiation emitted by the building. The *different colours indicate different temperatures*. The lighter colours are the hottest parts of the building. The coldest parts are blue.

Photographs like this are very useful to identify where heat is being lost from a building.

Photographs like this are very useful for identifying where heat is being lost from a building

Heat from the Sun

The transfer of heat by conduction or convection **requires particles**. The transfer of energy by radiation does not. There are no particles between the Sun and the Earth so heat cannot be transferred by conduction or convection. **Heat travels from the Sun to the Earth as waves (radiation).**

Heat which is transferred from the Sun by radiation is making this girl too hot

Absorption or reflection

When radiation strikes an object it can be either **absorbed** or **reflected**. Which one occurs depends upon the nature of the surface of the object.

Radiation can be reflected back into a room by placing a sheet of aluminium foil behind a radiator.

Radiation can be reflected back into a room by placing a sheet of aluminium foil behind the radiator

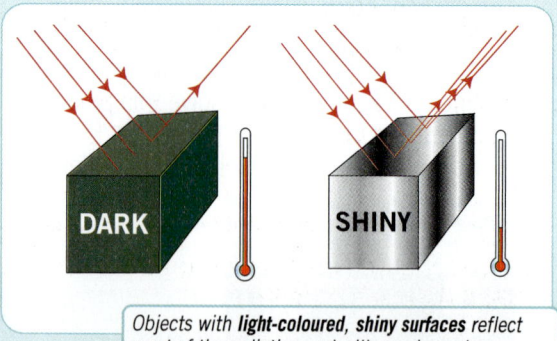

In hot countries where fuel is scarce, food can be cooked using a solar heater like the one shown below.

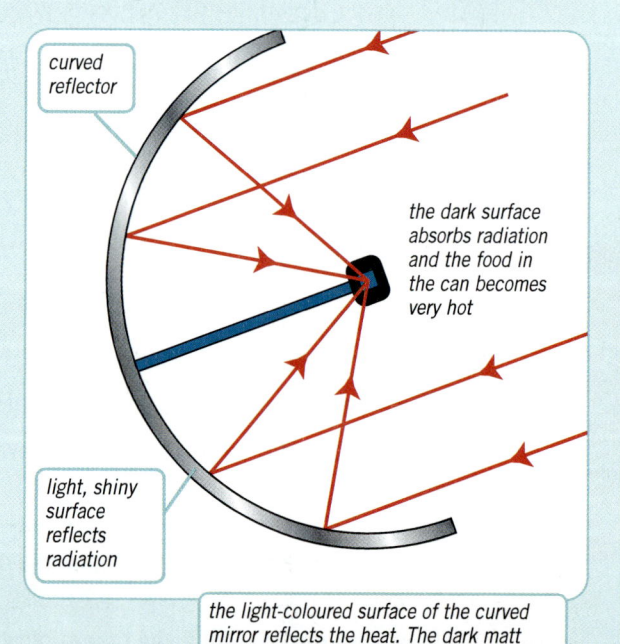

curved reflector

the dark surface absorbs radiation and the food in the can becomes very hot

light, shiny surface reflects radiation

*Objects with **light-coloured, shiny surfaces** reflect most of the radiation and will remain cooler*

the light-coloured surface of the curved mirror reflects the heat. The dark matt surface of the can absorbs the heat

Emitting radiation

How much radiation an object **emits** depends upon its temperature and the nature of its surface.

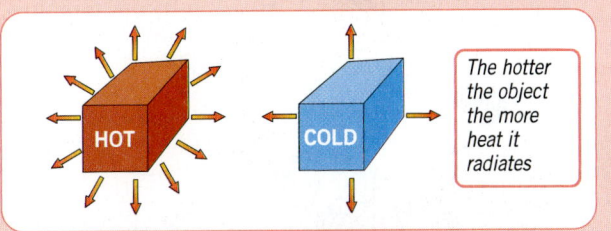

The hotter the object the more heat it radiates

Objects with **light, shiny surfaces** give off less radiation, i.e. they are **poor emitters**. Objects with **dark, matt surfaces** give off lots of radiation, i.e. they are **good emitters**.

When wrapped in these shiny space blankets, athletes will emit less radiation and so will lose body heat more slowly

We can demonstrate this with the 'tea pots experiment'. Both teapots are filled with hot water but after 20 minutes:

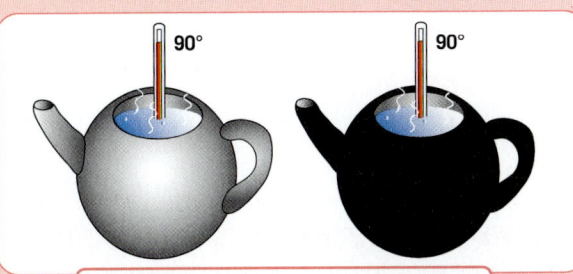

90°   90°

The water in the black teapot is cooler as it has emitted more radiation

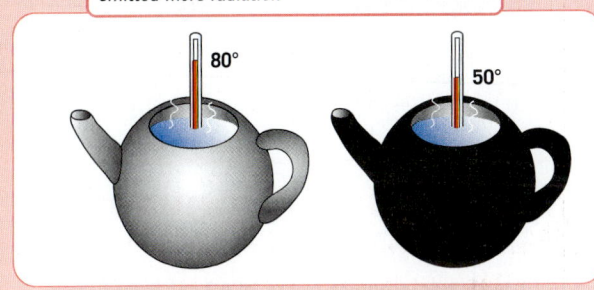

80°   50°

Heat transfer to and from bodies

The shape and size of a body affects the rate at which it gains or loses energy. The smaller the surface area, the lower the rate of heat transfer.

When animals are cold they try to curl up to reduce the surface area through which they are losing heat. When animals are too hot they try to stretch out to increase their surface area so that they can lose heat more quickly

Elephants have large bodies but with small surface areas so sometimes they can't get rid of heat quickly enough and become too hot. So what do they do with their ears?

> Remember that good **emitters** of radiation are also good **absorbers** of radiation.

KEY TERMS

Make sure you understand these terms before moving on!
- radiation
- radiates
- thermogram
- absorption
- reflection
- emits
- emitters
- absorbers

QUICK TEST

1. What kind of radiation is emitted by a hot object?
2. How do we know that heat travels from the Sun to Earth by radiation?
3. What two things might happen when radiation strikes an object?
4. What kind of a surface should an object, which is a good absorber of radiation, have?
5. What kind of a surface should an object, which is a poor absorber of radiation, have?
6. What is a thermogram?
7. Why might people in very hot, sunny countries paint their houses white?
8. How does the colour of the Artic and the Antarctic contribute to them being two of the coldest places on the Earth?

HEAT TRANSFER – RADIATION

Physics

Electrical power

All *electrical appliances* transfer *electrical energy* into *other forms*.

- A hairdryer transfers electrical energy into heat, kinetic and some sound energy.
- A radio transfers electrical energy into sound energy.

The *power* of an appliance is a measure of how quickly these energy *changes take place*. This *power rating* is *measured in watts*.

The meaning of power

If a light bulb has a **power rating of 40 W**, it transfers **40 J of electrical energy** into heat and light energy **every second**.

If an electrical fire has a **power rating of 2 kW** (2000 W) it **transfers 2000 J of electrical energy** into 2000 J of heat and light energy **every second**.

How many joules of energy have been transferred?
To calculate the total amount of energy an appliance has transferred we use the equation:

Energy = Power (in Watts) x time (in seconds) or E = P x t

Example
How much electrical energy is converted into heat and light energy when a 60 W bulb is turned on for 5 minutes?

E = P x t = 60 W x 300 s = 18 000 J or 18 kJ

Draw out the equation E = P x t as a formula triangle. Then try doing some problems where you have to find the values of P or t.

Kilowatt-hours and units

The electricity board measures the energy we use in the home in **kilowatt-hours** or **units**.

They calculate this value using the formula:

Energy used in kilowatt-hours = power in kilowatts x time in hours

Example
Calculate the energy used when a 3 kW fire is turned on for 2 h.

E = P x t = 3 kW x 2 h = 6 kWh or 6 units

The meter and the bill

- Somewhere in your house is a **meter** similar to the one shown above. It shows how many units of **electrical energy have been used**.
- We usually pay our electricity bills every three months, i.e. every quarter.
- By reading the meter at the beginning and end of the quarter we can calculate how many units of electrical energy have been used.
- The bill shows the **number of units used** and the **cost per unit**.
- By multiplying these two values together we can obtain the cost of the electrical energy used.
- The electricity company will also add to your bill a **standing charge**. This pays for the equipment used by the electricity company in bringing the electricity into your home and its maintenance.

Example

The readings on an electricity meter at the beginning and end of a quarter show that a family has used 800 units. If the cost of one unit is 11p and the standing charge per quarter is £12, calculate the total bill for this household.

Cost of electricity = number of units used x cost per unit = 800 x 11p = £88.00

If the standing charge is £12 the total cost of the bill is £88.00 + £12 = £100

ELECTRICITY BILL

Charges for electricity used

Present reading	Previous reading	Units used	Pence per unit	Charge amount
80139	78579	1560	11.00	£171.60

Quarterly standing charge	£12.00
Total	£183.60

ELECTRICAL POWER

Physics

KEY TERMS

Make sure you understand these terms before moving on!
- electrical appliances
- power
- watt (W)
- joule (J)
- kilowatt (kW)
- units

QUICK TEST

1. How many joules of electrical energy are used in the following situations?
   a) 100 W bulb turned on for one minute,
   b) 500 W computer and monitor on for five minutes,
   c) 600 W hairdryer turned on for two minutes,
   d) 1000 W heater turned on for four minutes and
   e) 2 kW tumble dryer turned on for five minutes.

2. How many kilowatt-hours (units) of electrical energy are converted into other forms in the following situations?
   a) 3 kW fire turned on for three hours,
   b) 2 kW tumble dryer used for 30 minutes,
   c) 1.5 kW water heater turned on for two hours,
   d) 500 W TV turned on for four hours and
   e) 100 W radio turned on for 10 hours.

3. The readings on an electricity meter at the beginning and end of a quarter show that a family has used 1200 units. If the cost of one unit is 12p and the standing charge per quarter is £10, calculate the total bill for this household.

Radiation/Waves

Radiation plays an important role in our lives. Most types of radiation can be both useful and hazardous. To take full advantage of their usefulness, but at the same time minimise the dangers, we need to understand them better.

What are waves?

Waves transfer energy by **vibrations**. There is no **transfer of particles**.

There are two main types of waves: **transverse waves** and **longitudinal waves**.

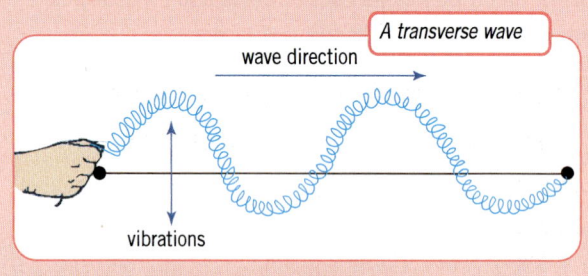

A transverse wave

A **transverse wave** has vibrations across or at right angles to the direction in which the wave is moving.

Examples of transverse waves include light waves and surface water waves.

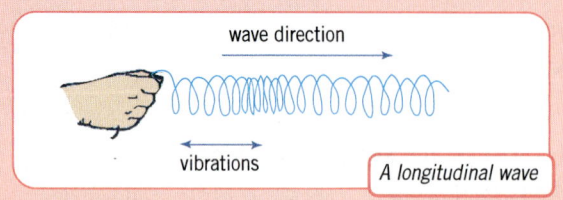

A longitudinal wave

A **longitudinal wave** has vibrations that are along the direction in which the wave is moving.

Sound waves are longitudinal waves.

The important bits

The **amplitude** of a wave is the height of a crest or depth of a trough from the undisturbed position.

The **wavelength** of a wave is the distance between successive crests.

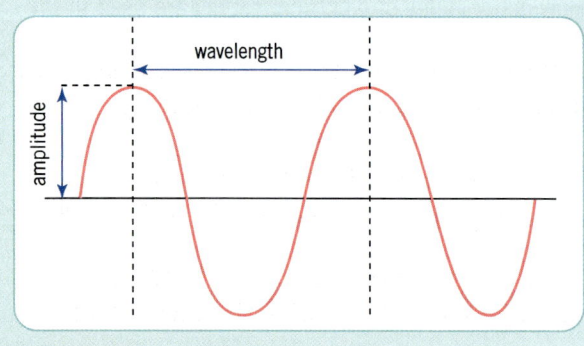

The **frequency** of a wave is the number of complete waves produced each second by the source. It is measured in hertz (Hz). A wave has a frequency of 200 Hz if the source is producing 200 waves each second.

We can also describe the frequency of a wave as being the number of waves which passes a point each second.

The velocity of a wave (v), its frequency (f) and its wavelength (λ) are related by the equation: **v = f x λ**

Example

A sound wave has a frequency of 170 Hz and a wavelength of 2 m. Calculate the velocity of this wave.

$$v = f \times \lambda = 170 \times 2 = 340 \text{ m/s}$$

Key properties of waves

- When a wave strikes a plane surface, it is **reflected** so that the angle of incidence is equal to the angle of reflection.
- When a wave travels across the boundary between two different mediums its speed and direction may change, i.e. the wave is **refracted**. If the wave slows, it is refracted towards the normal. If the wave speeds up, it is refracted away from the normal.
- If a wave travels from a more dense medium into a less dense medium and it strikes the boundary at an angle greater than the critical angle, the wave will be totally **internally reflected**.
- If a wave travels through a gap or across the edge of an object it may spread out. This process is called **diffraction** and is most noticeable if the size of the gap is the same as the wavelength of the wave.

The electromagnetic spectrum

Electromagnetic radiations are vibrations in an electric field. They travel as waves. This large **family of waves** has lots of **common properties**.

- They are all **able to travel through a vacuum**
- They all **travel at the same speed** through a vacuum, i.e. the speed of light
- They are all **transverse waves**
- They all **transfer energy**
- They can all be **reflected, absorbed, transmitted, refracted and diffracted**

Some of the **properties** of these waves **change** as their **wavelength and frequency** change. The family is therefore divided into seven smaller groups

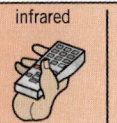

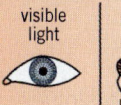

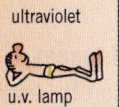

| long wavelength low frequency | radio waves | television | microwaves | infrared | visible light | ultraviolet u.v. lamp | X-rays | γ-rays, gamma rays | short wavelength high frequency |

Reflection, absorption and transmission

The amount of radiation which is reflected, absorbed or transmitted by an object depends upon:

- the type of radiation being used
- the material from which the object is made
- the nature of the surface of the object, i.e. is it shiny/dull etc?
- the time the object is exposed to the radiation

If radiation is absorbed the energy it carries may:

- warm the object
- produces cancerous changes
- kill living cells

Biological effects of exposure to electromagnetic waves

Radio waves	No known effect
Microwaves	These are absorbed by water molecules causing body tissue to warm. Large doses can cause burns. The rapid increase in the usage of mobile phones and the erection of microwave transmitter masts close to communities is causing concern over the possible long term effects of **exposure** to microwaves.
Infra red	Over exposure can cause burning to the skin.
Visible light	This causes the chemical changes on the retina of the eye which makes vision possible. Over exposure, e.g. looking directly at the Sun, can cause damage to the retina resulting in impaired vision or blindness.
Ultraviolet	These cause chemical changes in the skin resulting in tanning and premature aging. Excessive exposure will result in sunburn and possibly skin cancer. Sun blocks prevent all the radiation from reaching the skin.
X-rays	These are highly penetrating rays which can cause cancer and kill living cells. Workers exposed to X-rays, e.g. radiographers, wear lead aprons or stand behind lead screens, as X-rays cannot penetrate lead.
Gamma rays	Emitted by some radioactive materials, they are also very penetrating and can cause cancer and kill living cells.

KEY TERMS
- waves
- transverse wave
- longitudinal wave
- amplitude
- wavelength
- frequency
- electromagnetic spectrum
- transmission
- exposure

QUICK TEST
1. Give one example of a) a transverse wave and b) a longitudinal wave.
2. Name two properties all electromagnetic waves have in common.

The electromagnetic spectrum

Different members of the electromagnetic spectrum have different wavelengths and frequencies. They have therefore different properties or uses.

Radio waves

- Used for **communicating over large distances**.
- Short wavelength radio waves are used for television broadcasting and FM radio.
- Longer wavelength radio waves are used for traditional AM radio.
- When radio waves pass through a receiving aerial, signals (alternating currents) with the same frequencies are created. These waves/currents are processed to produce the final received signal.

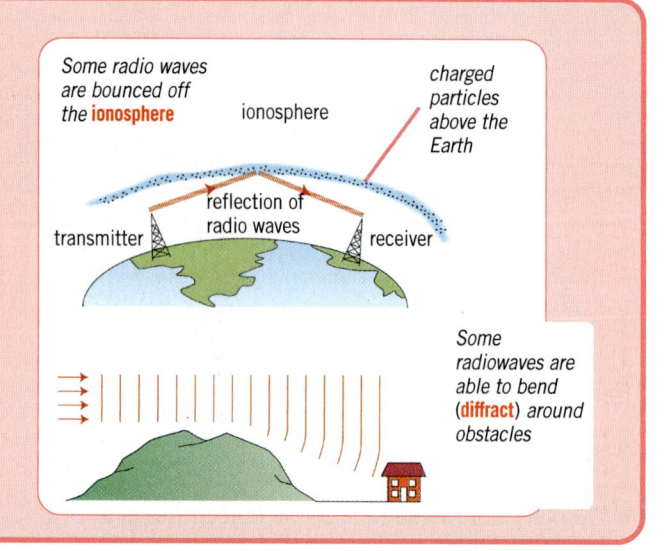

Some radio waves are bounced off the ionosphere

charged particles above the Earth

reflection of radio waves — transmitter — receiver

Some radiowaves are able to bend (diffract) around obstacles

Microwaves

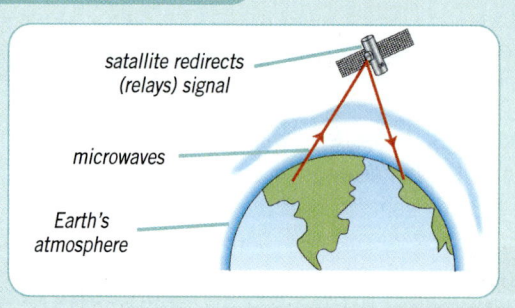

satellite redirects (relays) signal
microwaves
Earth's atmosphere

- Some microwaves pass easily through the Earth's atmosphere and so are used for **communications via satellites**, e.g. mobile phones.

- Some are used for **cooking**, e.g. **microwave ovens**.
- Water molecules inside food absorb microwaves.
- They become 'hot', cooking the food from the inside.

Microwaves can be dangerous if misused. They **can cause damage to living cells**.

food absorbs microwaves

Infrared waves (heat radiation)

- Infra-red waves are **given out by all objects**. The hotter they are, the more radiation they emit.
- Our skin can sense or detect the infra-red waves.
- Over exposure causes **sunburn, but not tanning**.
- Infra-red waves are used to 'see in the dark'. Special

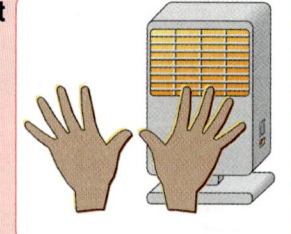

Warm objects give off infrared waves which our skin can detect

'heat seeking' cameras **create images** of objects **using the infrared waves they are emitting**. These are often used by the emergency services to detect people trapped in collapsed buildings or lost in mountains or on moors.

- **Remote controls** for TVs, radios, etc. use infra-red waves to carry instructions.

Infrared waves carry the instructions from the remote to the TV

Visible light

- We use these waves to see.
- It is the one part of the electromagnetic spectrum to which our **eyes are sensitive**.
- Visible light is used to carry messages down **optical fibres**.

We use visible light to see

X-rays

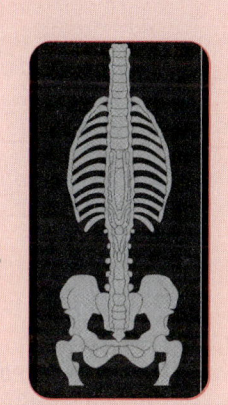

- X-rays have a very **short wavelength** and a very **high frequency**.
- They are **highly penetrating**.
- They are used to look for damaged bones inside the body.
- Over**exposure** can cause cancer. Radiographers therefore **stand behind lead screens** or **wear lead aprons** to **prevent overexposure**.
- They used to be used to monitor the development of the foetus in the womb during pregnancy, but ultrasound is used now as it is less likely to cause any damage to the unborn baby.

Gamma rays

- These are **very penetrating waves** which are **emitted by some radioactive materials**.
- Can be used to kill harmful bacteria, e.g. to sterilise surgical equipment.
- If used correctly they can be used to kill certain kinds of cancer, i.e. in radiotherapy.
- Incorrect exposure/**dosage** can **damage living cells** and **cause cancer**.

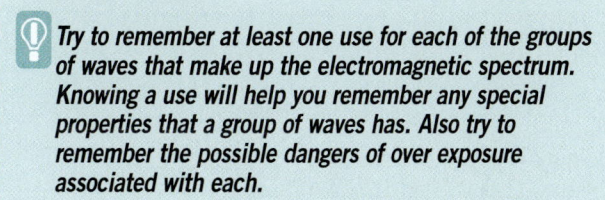

> *Try to remember at least one use for each of the groups of waves that make up the electromagnetic spectrum. Knowing a use will help you remember any special properties that a group of waves has. Also try to remember the possible dangers of over exposure associated with each.*

Ultraviolet

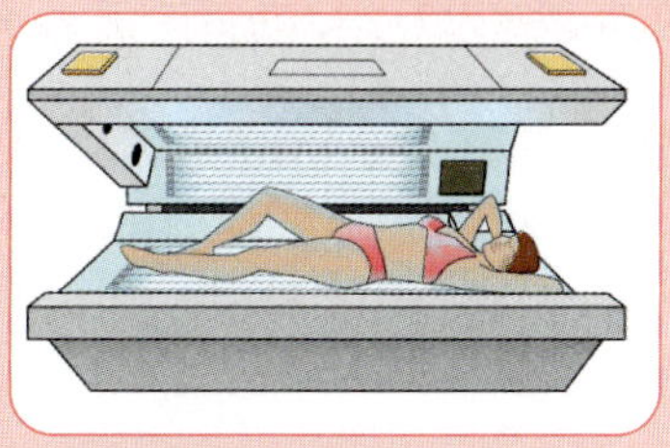

- Ultraviolet waves are **emitted by the sun**.
- They **cause our skins to tan**.
- Overexposure to ultraviolet waves **can lead to skin cancer**.
- Certain chemicals when exposed to ultraviolet **fluoresce** (glow).
- Words written with security markers are only visible in ultraviolet light.
- Ultraviolet light can be used to detect forged bank notes by fluorescence.

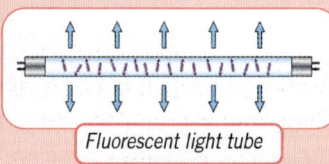

Fluorescent light tube

KEY TERMS

Make sure you understand these terms before moving on!
- ionosphere
- diffract
- fluoresce
- highly penetrating
- exposure
- dosage

QUICK TEST

1. Name three groups of waves that can be used for communications.
2. Name two groups of waves that can be used for cooking.
3. Name three groups of waves that might cause cancer.
4. Name one group of waves that can be used to treat cancer.
5. Name two types of waves we, as human beings, can sense.
6. Name one source of gamma waves.
7. Why are microwaves rather than radio waves used in satellite communication systems?
8. Why are X-rays no longer used to monitor the development of a foetus in the womb?

THE ELECTROMAGNETIC SPECTRUM

Physics

95

Analogue and digital signals

Most modern communication systems are using digital signals rather than the traditional analogue signals. This spread should help you understand why they are making these changes.

Total internal reflection and optical fibres

When a ray of light enters a glass block at an angle, it **slows down** and bends towards **the normal**. This change in direction is called **refraction**. When the ray emerges from the block it **speeds up** and bends **away from the normal**.

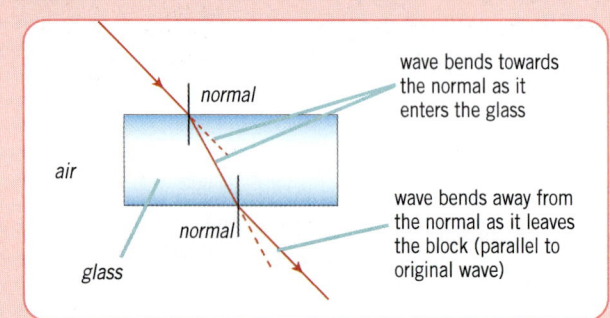

Total internal reflection in glass

If a ray leaving a glass block strikes the boundary at an angle **greater than the critical angle, total internal reflection** takes place, i.e. the ray is not refracted but reflected.

In modern telecommunications systems, **optical fibres** are being used to replace traditional **copper wires** to carry signals. The light signals in optical fibres undergo total internal reflection.

An optical fibre has a **high density glass for its core** and a **less dense glass as an outer coating**. The fibre is so narrow that light entering at one end will always strike the boundary between the two glasses at an angle greater than the critical angle. It will therefore undergo a **series of total internal reflections** before emerging at the far end.

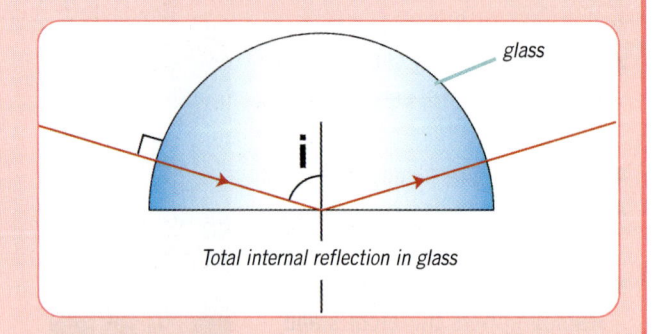

Advantages of using optical fibres:

- The fibres are cheaper than copper wires.
- They are lighter.
- They can carry more signals.
- The signals they carry are more secure.

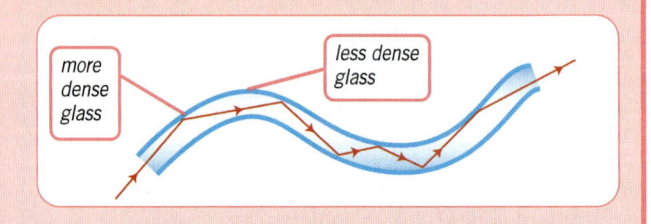

Communicating using analogue signals

As radio waves and microwaves travel from an emitter towards a receiver there may be some **loss in signal strength**. To ensure a strong signal arrives at the receiver it may be **amplified** several times at **repeater stations**.

Analogue signals vary continuously. When they are amplified at **repeater stations** any **distortions** (**noise**) which has been added to the wave during its journey will also be **amplified**. If the noise is considerable, the final signal received may be very different from the original and therefore difficult to understand.

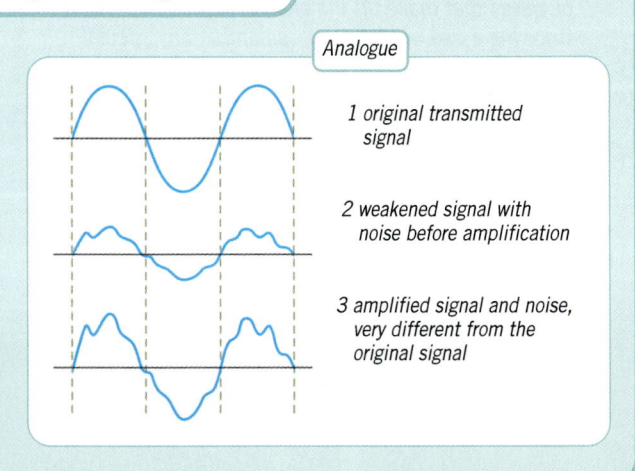

Analogue

1 original transmitted signal

2 weakened signal with noise before amplification

3 amplified signal and noise, very different from the original signal

Communicating using digital signals

Digital signals have only two values 1 and 0. An analogue signal can be converted into a digital signal, i.e. its continuously changing shape can be described by a **code consisting of just 1s and 0s**. This code can then be transmitted. When the weakened signal arrives at a repeater station it is easy to recognise, even with lots of noise, those parts of the signal which should be a 1 and those that should be a 0. These are processed and amplified, producing a **perfect copy of the original**. At the receiver, the digital code is converted back into the analogue signal, but without any noise distortion, i.e. the signal is very clear.

A second advantage of using digital signals is that they are already in a form which can be processed by computers.

💡 *The key things to remember here are the advantages in using digital signals rather than analogue.*

1 original signal which has been changed into a digital code before being transmitted

noise

2 weakened signal with noise before amplification

clean pulses

3 amplified signal which has had the original code restored, an exact copy of the original transmitted signal

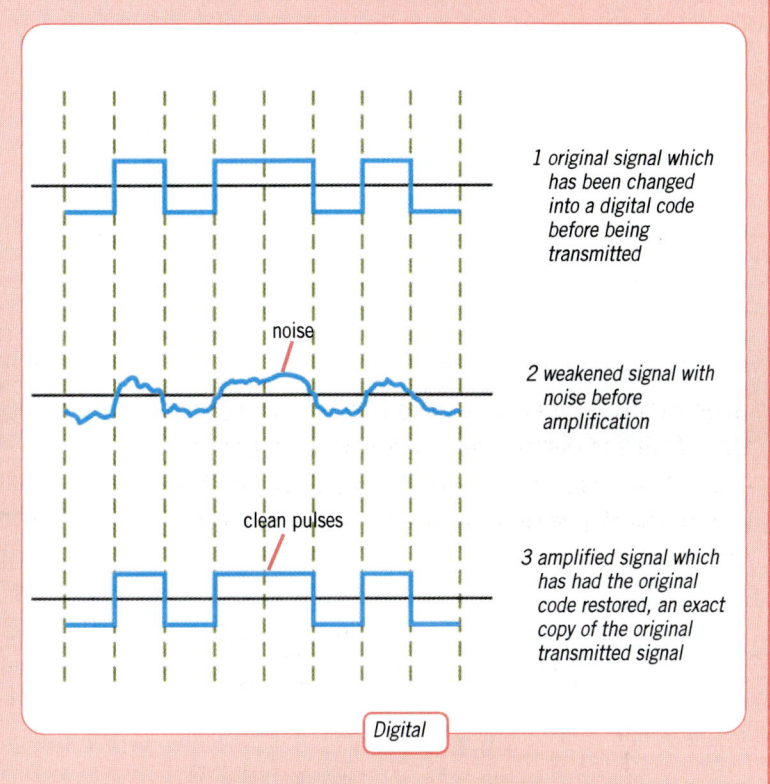

Digital

KEY TERMS

Make sure you understand these terms before moving on!
- refraction
- critical angle
- total internal reflection
- optical fibres
- repeater stations
- analogue signals
- digital signals
- noise

QUICK TEST

1. Why is light unable to escape through the sides of an optical fibre?
2. Name two different types of waves which might carry a signal along an optical fibre.
3. Give three reasons why optical fibres are replacing copper wires in telecommunications networks.
4. Why do signals need to pass through a repeater station?
5. What is noise?
6. How does noise affect an analogue signal?
7. What happens to the noise on an analogue signal when it passes through a repeater station? What effect does this have on the final signal received?
8. What is the main advantage of using digital signals rather than analogue?

Nuclear radiation

Some atoms have *unstable nuclei*. As a result they give out *radiation* all the time in order to become more stable. These substances are said to be *radioactive*. There are three types of radiation which might be emitted. These are called *alpha, beta and gamma* radiation.

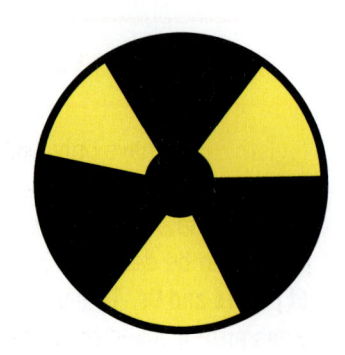

Radioisotopes

These nuclear radiations can be very useful. They can also be very dangerous. It is therefore important that we understand their properties.

It is the nuclei of atoms that emit different types of radiation

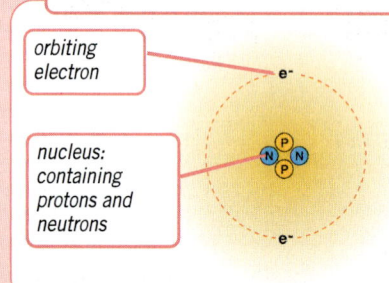

- orbiting electron
- nucleus: containing protons and neutrons

An atom has a central core called a nucleus which contains two types of particles called protons and neutrons. Very small particles called electrons orbit the nucleus.

All the nuclei of a particular element have the same number of protons. For example, all hydrogen atoms contain one proton in their nuclei, all helium atoms have two protons in their nuclei and all lithium atoms have three protons in their nuclei. We can get this information from a periodic table of elements similar to that on page 72.

Although the number of protons in the nucleus of an element is fixed, this is not always true for the number of neutrons. This can vary. For example, all chlorine atoms contain 19 protons in their nuclei, but some of them contain 18 neutrons and some contain 20 neutrons. These different forms of the same element are called **isotopes**. An isotope which gives out radiation is called a **radioisotope**.

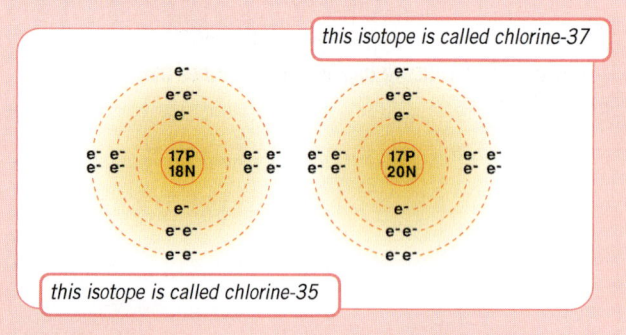

this isotope is called chlorine-37

this isotope is called chlorine-35

Before we have a look at some examples of radioisotopes and their uses it would be helpful to learn more about the radiations they emit. We will then be able to choose the correct radioactive source for a particular use.

Alpha radiation (α)

- Alpha particles are **slow moving helium nuclei**, i.e. they consist of **two protons and two neutrons**.
- They are **big and heavy** and so have **poor penetration** (just a few centimetres in air).
- They collide with lots of atoms **knocking some of their electrons off** and **creating ions**. They are **very good ionisers**.
- **An ion** is an atom which has become charged by either losing or gaining electrons.
- They are **positively charged** and so can be **deflected** by **electric and magnetic fields**.

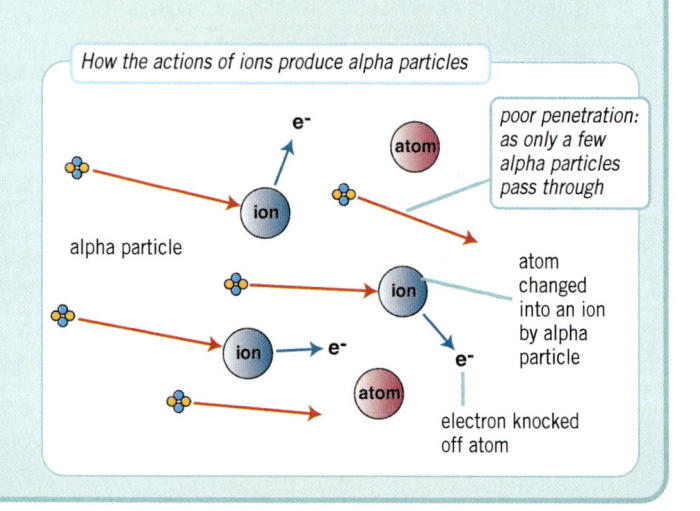

How the actions of ions produce alpha particles

poor penetration: as only a few alpha particles pass through

atom changed into an ion by alpha particle

electron knocked off atom

Beta radiation (β)

- These are **fast moving electrons**.
- They are small and therefore have quite good **penetrating powers** (up to about a metre in air).
- They do collide with atoms and produce ions but not as many as the alpha particles.
- They are **negatively charged** and so can be **deflected by electric and magnetic fields**.

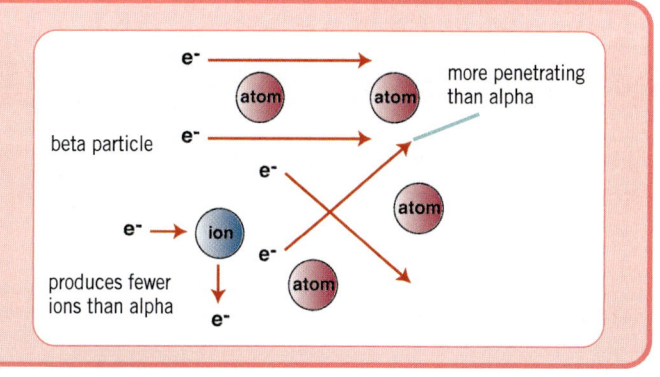

Gamma rays (γ)

- These are **short wavelength electromagnetic waves**, similar to X-rays.
- They **travel at the speed of light** and are **very penetrating**. (They can travel almost unlimited distances through air.)
- They do not hit many atoms as they travel through a material and so are **very poor ionisers**.
- Gamma radiation **carries no charge** and so is **unaffected by magnetic and electric fields**.

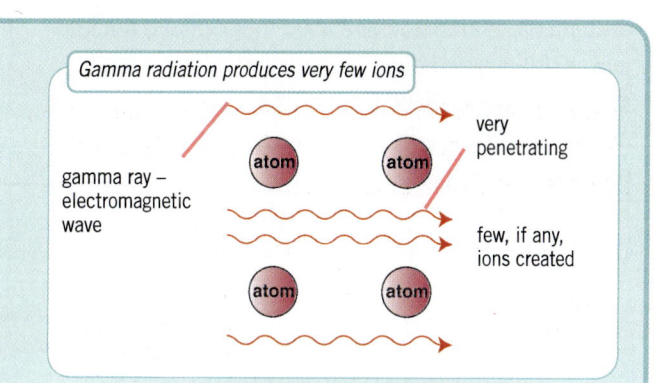

Comparison of the properties of alpha, beta and gamma radiation

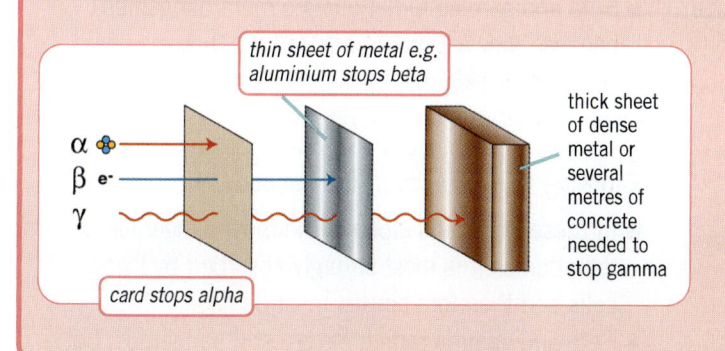

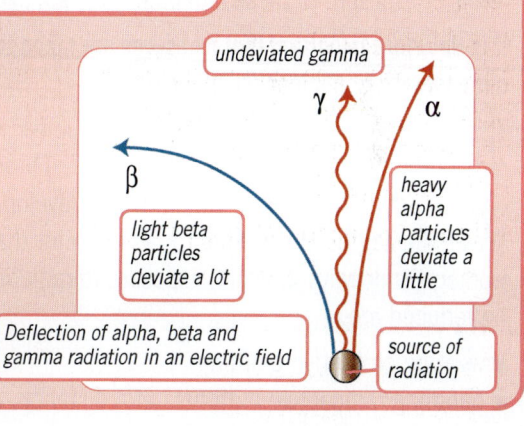

KEY TERMS

Make sure you understand these terms before moving on!
- unstable nuclei
- radioactive
- isotopes
- radioisotope
- ions
- ionisers
- deflected
- penetrating power

QUICK TEST

1. Name two particles found in the nuclei of atoms.
2. Why do some nuclei give out radiation?
3. What are isotopes?
4. What are radioisotopes?
5. Why is it important that we understand the properties of alpha, beta and gamma radiation?
6. Which type of radiation:
   a) is most penetrating?
   b) is the best ioniser?
   c) is negatively charged?
   d) is a fast moving electron?
   e) is an electromagnetic wave?

NUCLEAR RADIATION — Physics

Radioactivity and half life

This spread will help you understand where radioactivity come from, how it can affect us and how long it will last.

Sources of radioactivity

There are radioactive substances all around us. Some of them are man-made and used in hospitals, nuclear power stations and even in the home. Most of the radioactive substances around us are naturally occurring. They are in the ground, in the food we eat, they are even in the air we breathe. Some radiation reaches us from space. The radiation produced by these sources is called **background radiation**.

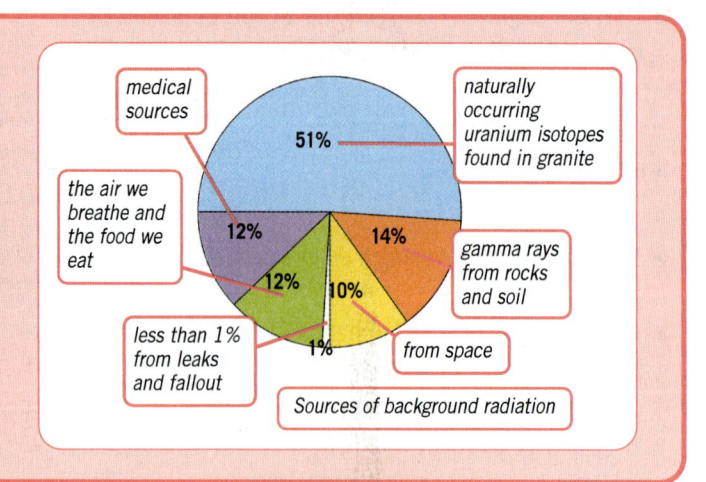

- medical sources
- naturally occurring uranium isotopes found in granite — 51%
- the air we breathe and the food we eat — 12%
- 14%
- gamma rays from rocks and soil
- 12%
- 10%
- less than 1% from leaks and fallout — 1%
- from space

Sources of background radiation

Exposure to radiation

Absorption of any of the three types of radiation by living cells is potentially dangerous. Absorption may cause **cell damage** and lead to illnesses such as **cancer**. Higher levels of exposure to these radiations may **kill living cells**.

It is therefore important that measures are taken to reduce our exposure to nuclear radiation.

Those at most risk, e.g. workers in the nuclear industry, radiographers, etc., wear **radiation badges**. These contain photographic film which, when developed, shows the **degree of exposure** to radiation for that worker. Other ways in which exposure to radiation can be reduced are:

- wearing protective clothing
- handling radioactive materials at a distance, e.g. using tongs
- limiting exposure time.

Nuclear radiation can pose real problems for us, both inside and outside our bodies.

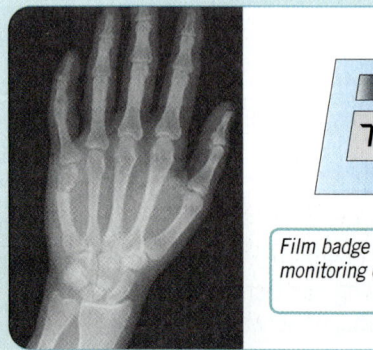

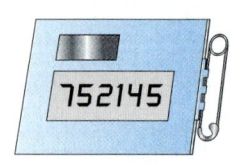

Exposure from sources outside the body

- In these situations, alpha radiation is the least dangerous as it is the least penetrating and unlikely to pass through the skin.
- Beta and gamma radiations are more dangerous because they are more penetrating. They may pass through the skin and cause cell damage inside the body.

Exposure from sources inside the body

- In these situations alpha is the most dangerous radiation as it is most strongly absorbed by living cells and therefore causes most damage.
- Beta and gamma radiations are still dangerous, but less so than alpha as they are less likely to be absorbed by living cells.

Film badge dosimeter for monitoring exposure to radiation

How long will the radioactivity last?

The **emission** of particles and waves from a nucleus is called **radioactive decay**. It is **impossible** to say exactly **when an individual nucleus will decay**. It is possible, however, to **estimate** how many **nuclei will decay** over a period of time.

Half life

- The **amount of radiation emitted each second** by a radioisotope – its **activity** – depends upon **how many unstable nuclei are present**.
- As time goes by, the **number of unstable nuclei** in a sample **decreases**.
- The **activity of a source** therefore **decreases with time**.
- We describe this decrease using the idea of a **half life**.

The half life of a radioactive material is the average time for the number of un-decayed nuclei in a sample of material to halve.

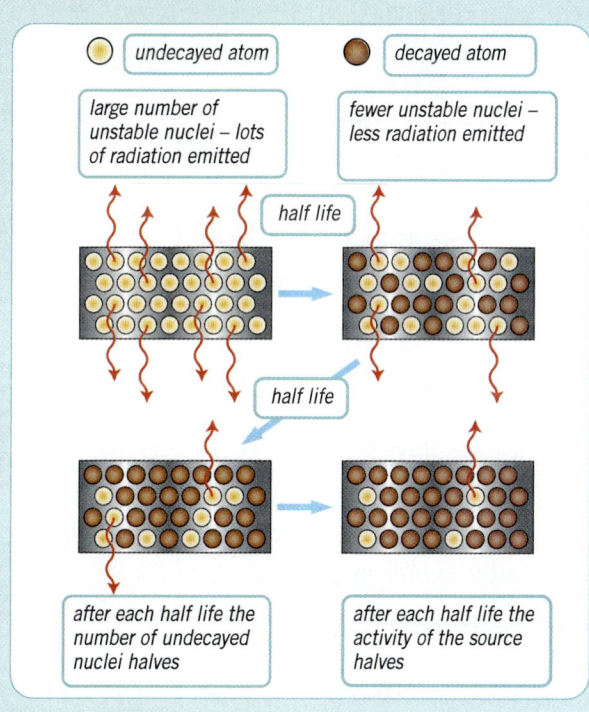

Different radioactive materials have different half lives. Here are some examples:

Isotope	Half life
Uranium-238	4500 million years
Radium-226	1620 years
Strontium-90	28 days
Randon-222	4 days
Radium-214	20 minutes

If we know the half life of a radioactive material we can calculate/estimate how the radiation it emits will decrease with time. This can be important when considering a radioisotope for a particular purpose. For example, any radioisotope which is introduced into the body should have quite a short half life so that the overall dosage it delivers does not cause damage to living cells.

Example 1

The initial activity of a radioisotope is 960 decays per second. If the half life of the isotope is 20 minutes, calculate the activity of the source after a) one hour and b) one hour 40 minutes.

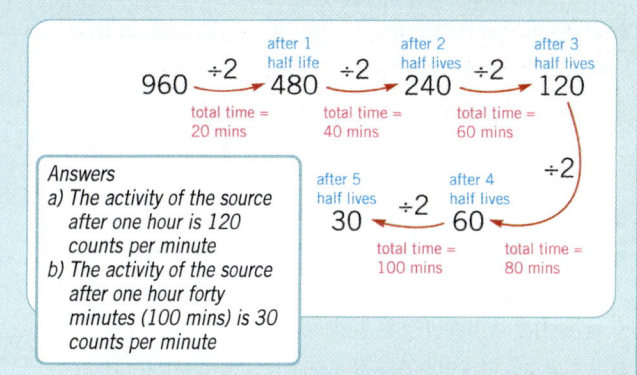

$960 \xrightarrow{\div 2} 480 \xrightarrow{\div 2} 240 \xrightarrow{\div 2} 120 \xrightarrow{\div 2} 60 \xrightarrow{\div 2} 30$

Answers
a) The activity of the source after one hour is 120 counts per minute
b) The activity of the source after one hour forty minutes (100 mins) is 30 counts per minute

Example 2

A radioisotope initially contains 8×10^8 un-decayed nuclei. After six days it contains 1×10^8 un-decayed nuclei. Calculate the half life of the isotope.

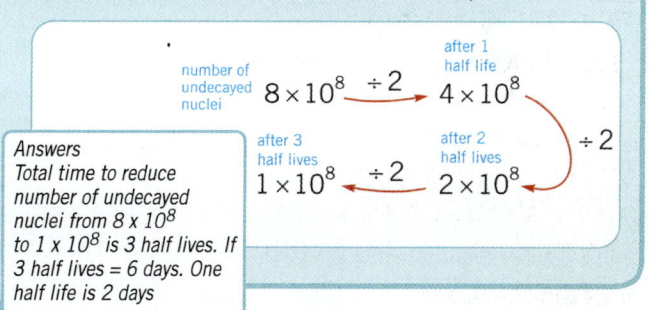

$8 \times 10^8 \xrightarrow{\div 2} 4 \times 10^8 \xrightarrow{\div 2} 2 \times 10^8 \xrightarrow{\div 2} 1 \times 10^8$

Answers
Total time to reduce number of undecayed nuclei from 8×10^8 to 1×10^8 is 3 half lives. If 3 half lives = 6 days. One half life is 2 days

KEY TERMS
- background radiation
- radiation badges
- radioactive decay
- activity
- half life

QUICK TEST

1. Name three sources of radioactivity which contribute to background radiation.
2. Give one example of the kind of workers whose exposure to radiation must be carefully monitored.
3. Which type of radiation is most damaging when emitted from a source which is inside the body?
4. The activity of a radioisotope drops from 600 decays per second to 150 decays per second in 6 days. Calculate its half life.
5. A radioisotope has a half life of 4 minutes. How long will it take for 7/8ths of a sample of the isotope to decay?

Uses of radioactivity

Now we have a good understanding of the different properties of alpha, beta and gamma radiation and the half life of a radioisotope, we can look for a source most suited to a particular job. Some examples of the different uses we have for radioisotopes are described below.

Quality control

- **Sheet material**, such as paper, needs to be produced with a **constant thickness**.
- This can be monitored using the emissions from a radioactive source.
- In this situation a beta emitting source with a long half life such as strontium-90 is placed above the paper.
- A **beta detector** is placed directly beneath it.
- If the paper becomes thinner, more radiation reaches the detector and the control system decreases the pressure between the rollers.
- If the paper becomes thicker, less radiation is detected and the pressure on the rollers is increased.
- **Continuous monitoring** like this guarantees that the thickness/quality of the paper is correct.

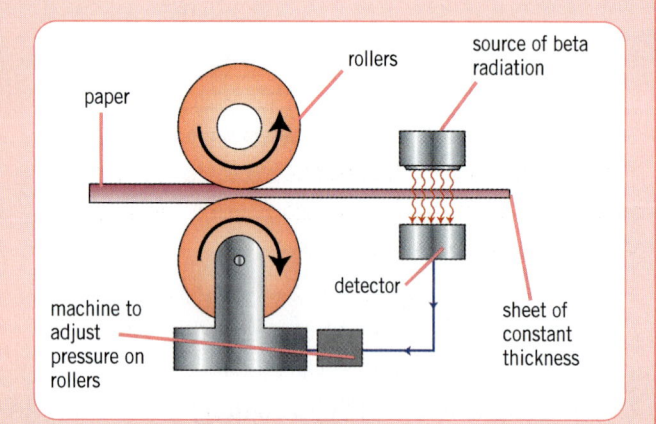

- This arrangement can also be used to monitor the quality of **sheet metal**, but now we would have to find a gamma emitting source with a long half life to replace the strontium-90.

Radioactive tracers

Radioisotopes can be used to monitor the flow of **liquids and gases in pipes**.

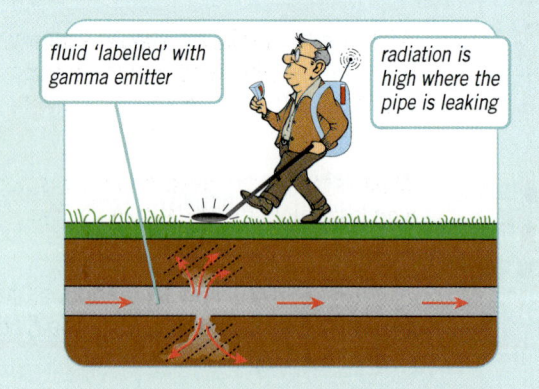

- If the pipe is underground, a gamma emitting radioisotope is added to the fluid flowing through it. This material is called a **tracer**.
- If there is **a leak** in the pipe a **higher concentration** of gamma radiation will be detected.
- Using a radioisotope in this manner **avoids the need to dig up whole sections** of roads and piping in order to find the leak.
- Tracers can also be used to check the progress of fluids such as blood and digested food through the body. For example, sodium-24 is a radioisotope that can be introduced into the body to check for **internal bleeding**.

Radiotherapy

Some forms of cancer can be removed by surgery. Others, like brain tumours, because of their position, may require a different solution, e.g. **radiotherapy**.

- Narrow beams of radiation are directed at the **tumour** from different positions.
- A **high dose of radiation** needed to kill the cancerous cells only occurs within the tumour.
- In other places the dose is not large enough to cause cell damage.

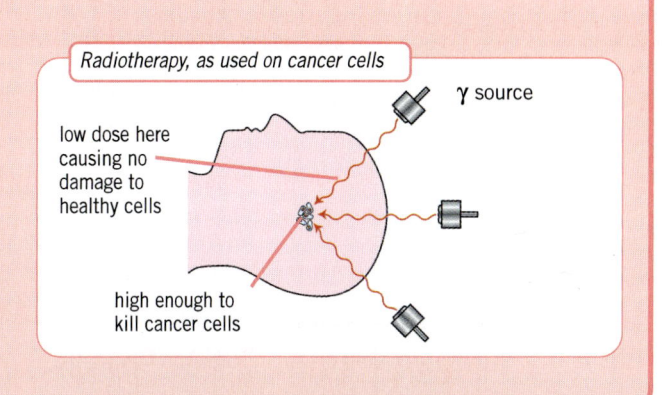

Radiotherapy, as used on cancer cells

γ source
low dose here causing no damage to healthy cells
high enough to kill cancer cells

Sterilisation

Food rots because of the presence and growth of bacteria. Cooling and freezing slows down the growth of the bacteria but does not prevent it.

If food is exposed to gamma radiation before being frozen, the bacteria are killed and the food keeps for much longer. This process is called **sterilisation**.

Surgical instruments used to be sterilised by putting them in boiling water. Nowadays, these instruments are sterilised by exposing them to gamma radiation.

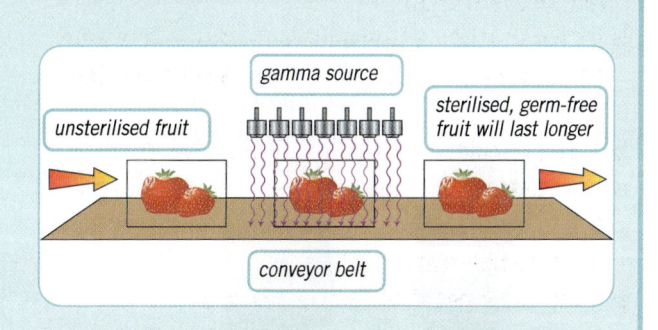

gamma source
unsterilised fruit
sterilised, germ-free fruit will last longer
conveyor belt

Smoke detectors

Some **smoke detectors**, like the one shown here, contain a small amount of americium-241. This is an **alpha emitter**. The alpha particles emitted collide with air molecules within the smoke detector **creating ions**. This in turn creates a **very small current**. If smoke enters the detector this **current stops or decreases**. It is this change in current which **triggers the alarm**.

One big advantage of this type of smoke detector is that when the battery is towards the end of its life, this too causes the current to fall and the alarm to sound, indicating that the battery needs replacing.

💡 *This is a very popular topic in exams. Make sure you can explain some of these uses.*

KEY TERMS

- quality control
- tracer
- radiotherapy
- sterilisation
- smoke detectors
- creating ions

QUICK TEST

1. What kind of radiation should a source emit if it is to be used for monitoring the thickness of a) card and b) sheets of steel?
2. What is the name given to a radioisotope which is injected into a fluid so that its flow can be monitored?
3. Why should a source which emits alpha radiation not be used to check the flow of blood through a body?
4. What is the treatment of cancer with radiation called?
5. Which type of radiation is used to sterilise surgical instruments?
6. What causes a current to flow in a smoke detector?

USES OF RADIOACTIVITY — Physics

Our universe

- Did our universe have a beginning or did it always exist?
- Will our universe have an end or will it continue to exist forever?

Scientists and philosophers have been trying to answer these questions for a long time. We now have two clues which may help us provide an answer.

Red shift

I hear a note which is higher than normal so I know the motorbike is approaching.

The note from the engine is now lower than normal, so I know the motorcycle is moving away.

The **change in frequency heard** by the man allows him to identify which **way the motorcycle is moving** even though his eyes are shut.

Astronomers see similar changes when they look at the light from distant stars and galaxies. Their light, when compared with light from a stationary star, seems to be stretched, i.e. its frequency is less and its wavelength is longer. This is called **red shift**.

If this is repeated with light from a very distant **galaxy** the red shift is **even greater**, i.e. it is moving away from us at an even faster rate.

This is precisely the **pattern of movements** we observe after an **explosion** and it suggests that at one time in the past **all the matter** in the universe was **in one place**, but it was then scattered outwards by a huge explosion scientists call the **Big Bang**. This suggests that the universe **is expanding**.

Light from stationary star

Light from star moving away is stretched

Cosmic background radiation

When an explosion takes place, energy is released, often in the form of heat and kinetic energy. Gradually the hotter objects will lose some of their energy to the surroundings causing it to become slightly warmer.

Scientists in the 1960s detected energy in the form of **background microwaves** (cosmic background radiation) in all parts of the Universe. They believe that this radiation is the remains of the energy released during the Big Bang.

Scientists are now asking the question: 'Will this expansion continue indefinitely or will gravity gradually slow it down and then perhaps reverse the process, pulling all matter back to one place (**The Big Crunch**)?'

Perhaps then there may be another explosion and the whole process will begin again (**The Oscillating Model of the Universe**). The total amount of matter in the Universe will determine its future. Whilst trying to measure how much matter there is in the Universe, scientists have discovered a new phenomenon called **dark matter** and it may be its presence that decides our fate.

The model of the Universe is a good example of how science and scientific ideas evolve. The more we explore space, the more we discover and this often makes us rethink some of our previous conclusions.

> *Try to remember that two key observations suggest how our universe began—red shift and left over background energy from the explosion.*

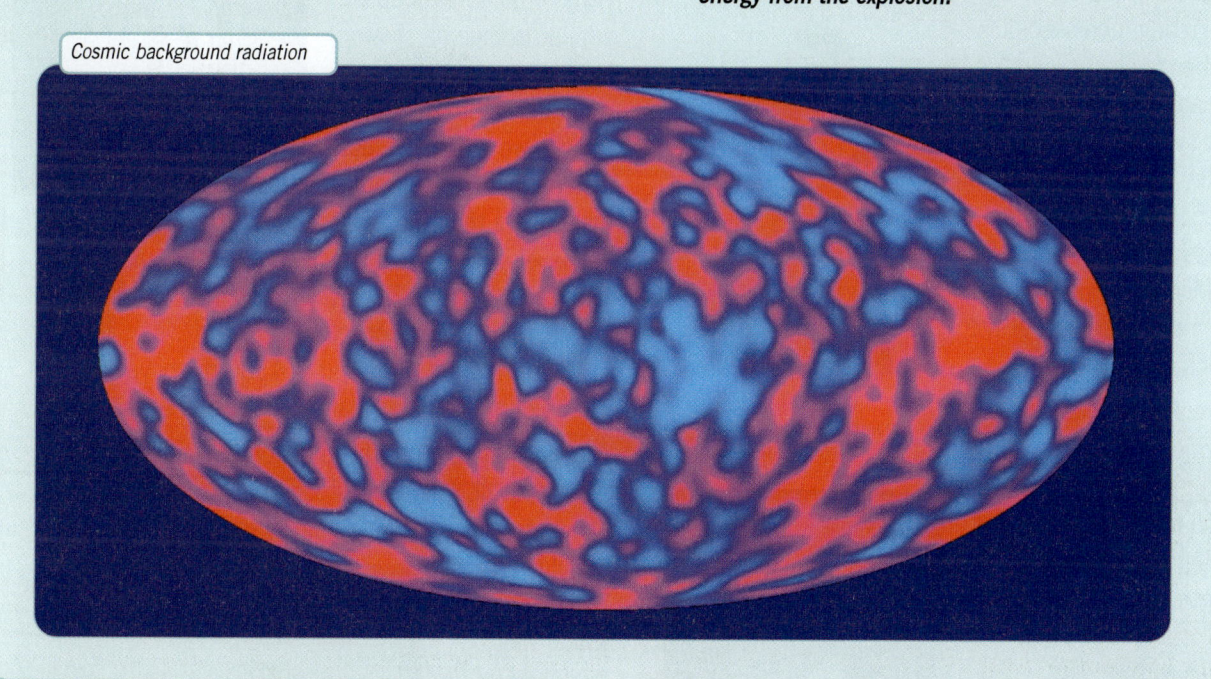

Cosmic background radiation

KEY TERMS

Make sure you understand these terms before moving on!
- red shift
- galaxy
- Big Bang
- cosmic background radiation
- The Big Crunch

QUICK TEST

1. What happens to the frequency of the noise made by a motorcycle as it approaches and then passes an observer?
2. How does light appear if it is emitted by an object that is moving away from us very quickly?
3. What is this phenomenon called?
4. How does the red shift from a distant galaxy compare with that from a very distant galaxy? What conclusions can you draw from this?
5. How was matter in the universe distributed in the beginning, according to the Big Bang theory?
6. Describe two possible futures for our Universe.

Exploring space

Apart from the Earth and the Moon, humans have not visited any of the other bodies in the Universe. Nevertheless, we have lots of information about them. Much of this has come from observations made by *telescopes* and *probes*.

Telescopes

Before the invention of telescopes, all human observations were done with the **unaided eye**. Our view of the universe was very limited. **Optical telescopes** first appeared in the 1570s and greatly increased our abilities to see new astronomical bodies in our solar system. In 1609, Galileo used an optical telescope to discover the valleys and mountains of the Moon. He was also the first man to see four of the moons of Jupiter.

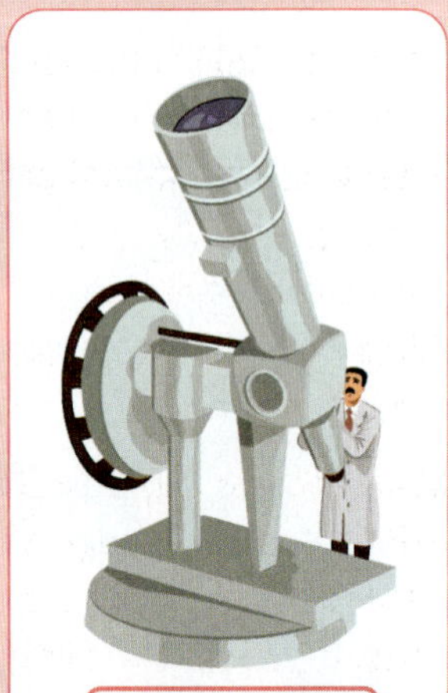

There are two main types of optical telescope. These are **refracting telescopes**, which use **lenses** to gather the light and create images, and **reflecting telescopes**, which use **curved mirrors**. The reflecting telescope was invented by Sir Isaac Newton in 1671.

Most observatories use reflecting telescopes because:

- they do not suffer from **chromatic aberration**, i.e. there is no rainbow-type colouring added to the image

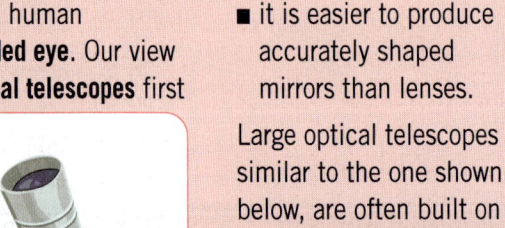

- it is easier to produce accurately shaped mirrors than lenses.

Large optical telescopes similar to the one shown below, are often built on mountain tops. Here the images we see suffer less **distortions** from the **Earth's atmosphere** than those at sea level. Also there is less **light pollution**. The largest optical telescope in the world is in Hawaii, it is 4300 m above sea level on top of an extinct volcano called Mauna Kea.

Another way to avoid these distortions is to mount **telescopes on satellites**, which orbit the Earth high above its atmosphere. A good example of this is the **Hubble Telescope**, which was launched in 1990. It has seen **further into space** than any previous telescope.

Refracting telescope

Reflecting telescope

The Hubble Telescope orbiting the Earth. It is able to see further into space and obtain clearer images than any earthbound telescope

This photograph taken by the Hubble Telescope shows a region in space which is 210 000 light years away. It is of great interest because stars are being formed here

Probes

Telescopes have also been sent into space on **probes**. Often these telescopes can send back images from view-points which are just not possible from Earth. Also, because they are closer to a body, they can make far more detailed observations.

The probe Deep Space 1 was launched in 1998 to fly close to a large asteroid called Braille and study its surface

Making observations using other parts of the electromagnetic spectrum

Until the 20th century, we learned about our universe by studying visible light which was emitted or reflected from astronomical objects. In 1932 it was discovered that many astronomical objects emitted radio waves, so astronomers developed **radio telescopes** which use large dishes to collect and focus these signals. Once they have been processed and analysed by computers, images can be created.

Many objects in space do not emit enough visible light to be visible when using an optical telescope. They may, however, emit enough radio waves to be visible using a radio telescope similar to the one shown

A major advantage of using **radio telescopes** is that radio waves are **unaffected by sunlight, cloud or rain**. Also, in order to gather more information, it is possible to link a large number of small dishes.

Astronomers now use telescopes which gather information from space using other parts of the **electromagnetic spectrum**. These include infrared telescopes, microwave telescopes, ultraviolet telescopes, X-ray telescopes and gamma ray telescopes. Each of the images created by these different telescopes adds to our understanding of the universe.

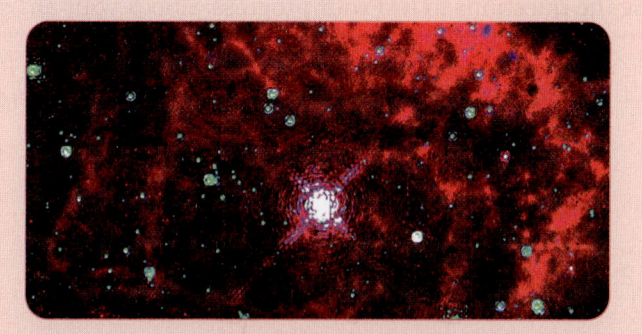

This photograph above taken with the Hubble Telescope, shows the importance of observing the universe using different parts of the electromagnetic spectrum. The star in the middle of the photograph is in the centre of our galaxy. It cannot be seen using visible light as it is obscured by clouds of interstellar dust, but using infrared it is clearly visible.

Although there may be advantages in using different parts of the electromagnetic spectrum to make observations, there are disadvantages too. **Gamma rays, X-rays, ultraviolet and some infrared are dramatically affected by the Earth's atmosphere.** Telescopes which use these waves, therefore, must always be sited high above the ground or in space.

KEY TERMS

Make sure you understand these terms before moving on!
- refracting telescopes
- reflecting telescopes
- chromatic aberration
- light pollution
- probes
- radio telescope
- electromagnetic spectrum

QUICK TEST

1. Describe the main difference between a refracting telescope and a reflecting telescope.
2. Why do most observatories use reflecting telescopes?
3. Who was the first man to see mountains on the Moon?
4. Who invented the first reflecting telescope?
5. Give two reasons why some telescopes are sited on top of mountains.
6. Name four other parts of the electromagnetic spectrum which could be used to 'observe' space, apart from visible light.
7. Name a telescope which is sited in space.
8. Give one advantage of observing a body using a radio telescope.

Practice questions

Use the questions to test your progress. Check your answers on page 112.

1. Name a device which transforms electrical energy into

    a) gravitational potential energy ....

    b) kinetic energy. ....

2. a) Name three fossil fuels.

    Coal oil gas

    b) Why are fossil fuels called non-renewable sources of energy?
    ....

    c) Name a fuel which is renewable.
    ....

    d) Suggest three ways in which the rate at which fossil fuels are being used could be reduced.
    ....

3. Explain what is meant by the phrase 'renewable source of energy'. Name three renewable sources of energy.
    ....

4. A crane uses 500 J of electrical energy to give a crate 300 J of gravitational potential energy. Calculate the efficiency of the crane. Suggest where the other 200 J of energy go.
    ....

5. A compact fluorescent light is 15% efficient. How much electrical energy must enter this device in order to produce 450 J of light energy?
    ....

6. a) What energy transfers take place in a coal fired power station?
    ....

    b) Describe two ways in which the atmosphere is polluted when coal is burned.
    ....

7. This diagram shows a hydroelectric power station.

    a) What kind of energy does the water possess in the top lake?
    ....

    b) What kind of energy does the water possess as it enters the turbine?
    ....

    c) Explain how surplus energy could be stored until it is needed.
    ....

    d) Calculate the efficiency of a turbine which transfers 800 kJ of energy into 600 kJ of electrical energy every second.
    ....

8. Calculate the electrical energy used in units when a 2 kW fire is turned on for 3 hours. Calculate the cost of this energy if the cost of one unit is 11p.

9. Calculate the total electrical energy used in units when the following devices are used

   a) a 2 kW fire for 2 hours ....

   b) a 500 W TV for 6 hours..

   c) a 2 kW washing machine for 30 minutes. ....

10. Calculate the payback time for each of the following methods of insulating your home using the information in the table below.

Type of insulation	Cost	Annual saving
draft excluders	£50	£25
double glazing	£900	£60
cavity wall insulation	£600	£75
insulating the loft	£150	£50

11. Why are very small birds, such as wrens, more likely to die during a harsh winter than bigger ones such as blackbirds?

12. The diagram below shows the electromagnetic spectrum.

| A | Microwaves | Infrared | Visible light | Ultraviolet | X-rays | B |

   a) Name the groups of waves A and B.

   b) Name two differences between the groups A and B.

   c) Name two groups that could be used for cooking.

   d) Name three groups that could be used for communicating.

13. Calculate the frequency of a sound wave with a wavelength of 0.4 m. Speed of sound is 340 m/s.

14. Which type of radiation is causing concern because of the increase in usage of mobile phones?

15. Give two advantages of using digital signals rather than analogue signals.

16. Name three medical uses for radioisotopes.

Answers

Biology
Quick test answers

Page 5 The nervous system
1. Skin, tongue, eyes, ears, and nose
2. Central nervous system
3. The brain, spinal cord and nerves
4. Sensory, relay and motor neurone
5. A gap between neurones that transmits the nerve impulse
6. Sensory neurone
7. Motor neurone
8. Relay neurone
9. True
10. By a chemical diffusing across a synapse between neurones

Page 7 The reflex arc
1. Brain or spinal cord
2. 3
3. A stimulus or change in the environment
4. Yes
5. To protect us from harm
6. Reflex actions are automatic, voluntary actions you have to think about
7. Yes, for example if you are holding a really expensive hot plate and can't drop it until you reach the table where you can put it down
8. The receptor detects the stimulus
9. Motor neurone
10. Sensory neurone

Page 9 The menstrual cycle
1. In the bloodstream
2. Lack of progesterone
3. Ovaries
4. Ovaries
5. FSH
6. Luteinising hormone(LH) and follicle stimulating hormone(FSH)
7. Development of an egg and release of oestrogen
8. Progesterone and oestrogen
9. Release of an egg
10. In vitro fertilisation

Page 11 A balanced diet
1. Energy
2. Starch and glucose
3. Starch carbohydrate
4. Fats
5. For insulation, for storing energy and for making cell membranes
6. It helps repair or replace damaged cells
7. It helps food move smoothly through your system
8. Glycogen
9. Vitamins and minerals
10. Cholesterol

Page 13 Nutrition and health
1. Increased blood cholesterol which can lead to heart disease
2. Polyunsaturated fats
3. 6 g
4. 0.1g
5. Protein
6. High metabolic rate
7. In the liver
8. Heart disease, arthritis, diabetes, high blood pressure
9. Eat limes, oranges and lemons
10. Adolescent females as they lose blood every month during their period

Page 15 Causes of disease
1. Virus, bacteria and fungi
2. Pathogens or germs
3. Mosquitoes carry malaria
4. They reproduce inside living cells and kill them
5. Athlete's foot and ringworm
6. Circular DNA inside bacteria
7. An organism that transports a diseases from person to person, e.g. mosquito
8. Skin, digestive, reproductive and respiratory systems and vectors
9. A virus
10. Food poisoning, tuberculosis, cholera

Page 17 Defence against disease
1. It's a barrier and produces an antiseptic oil
2. It traps dust and germs
3. Sterilising, disinfectants, antiseptics and good hygiene
4. Phagocytes and lymphocytes
5. They engulf them
6. Antitoxins and antibodies
7. Destroy toxins
8. Attach to antigens and clump germs together for the phagocytes to engulf
9. Because your body produces antibodies the first time you get the disease which remain in your body and fight the disease and destroy it before symptoms develop
10. They contain antigens on their surface

Page 19 Treatment of disease
1. Measles, mumps and rubella
2. The fact that it is three vaccines in one injection
3. Penicillin
4. They mutate
5. Viruses invade the hosts' own cells so to try to kill them using antibiotics would mean harming the bodies' own cells
6. Dead or harmless forms of the disease
7. Where neither the doctor nor the patient knows whether they are receiving the drug being tested
8. A dummy drug not containing the active ingredient being tested and will not have any affect on the patient
9. Because it caused birth defects in babies born to mothers taking the drug
10. Vaccinations are passive as they cause the body to make their own antibodies

Page 21 Drugs
1. Brain, liver and nervous system
2. Class C
3. Tar, nicotine and carbon monoxide
4. Emphysema, bronchitis, lung cancer and heart diseases
5. Cirrhosis

Page 23 Genetic engineering
1. A plasmid
2. Genetically modified
3. By using enzymes
4. They could develop resistance to herbicides or insecticides
5. Cystic fibrosis, diabetes etc.
6. They could be grown in cold countries throughout the year
7. The pancreas
8. Making insulin or human growth hormone
9. They may mutate into harmful bacteria
10. The use of genetic engineering to treat inherited diseases

Page 25 Genes
1. Chromosomes
2. Proteins and enzymes
3. Sections of DNA that code for a particular characteristic
4. On the chromosomes
5. If they occur in reproductive cells
6. 46, in the nucleus
7. 2
8. Sperms and eggs
9. Asexual reproduction
10. Sexual reproduction and the environment

Page 27 Selective breeding
1. Breeding animals and plants together to produce the best offspring
2. Artificial selection involves humans doing the selecting rather than nature
3. Genetically identical individuals
4. Embryo transfer
5. Taking cuttings and tissue culture
6. A reduction in the number of alleles
7. Asexual reproduction
8. Lots of cows and bulls can be produced from just one bull and one cow

Page 29 Evolution
1. 3 billion years ago
2. Charles Darwin
3. Environmental change, competition, disease and predators
4. The best adapted
5. Natural selection/survival of the fittest
6. Galapagos Islands off the coast of South America
7. A group of individuals that can breed together to produce fertile offspring
8. He saw that they all showed variation
9. There were more offspring produced than could survive
10. Evolution is a gradual process

Page 31 Evidence for evolution
1. The ground changed from marshy land to hard ground
2. The dark form; camouflaged against predators
3. Oxygen, moisture and warmth
4. They are unable to adapt
5. The remains of dead organisms that have not decayed and who lived millions of years ago
6. Yes because there is an absence of warmth
7. Mutation
8. By destroying habitats, hunting or pollution
9. Near the surface with older fossils further down
10. Natural Selection

Page 33 Adaptation and competition
1. Where an organism lives
2. The living things in a habitat
3. Animals or plants
4. Food, water and space
5. Light, space, water and nutrients
6. Also increase at first
7. Because of the predator prey cycle
8. White (camouflage), thick (insulation) and greasy (doesn't hold water)

Page 35 Environmental damage
1. Improved health care, medicine and agriculture
2. Problems in food chains
3. Washed in by rain
4. Eutrophication
5. Building, farming, dumping rubbish and quarrying
6. Cutting down of trees and forests
7. Less carbon dioxide is being absorbed
8. Soil erosion, less rainfall and the destruction of habitats
9. Manure
10. Organic farming, greenhouses and alternative energy sources

Answers to Practice questions
Page 36
1. Fertilisers or sewage getting washed into rivers and lakes
2. A sleeping pill
3. Using the best bull sperm and the best cow eggs, fertilising them and implanting them into surrogate cows
4. Dolly was the first mammal to be cloned
5. Developing world where the diets are deficient in protein
6. It deprives the foetus of oxygen and leads to a low birth weight
7. Nowhere - it's extinct!
8. Active immunity is when the body fights off a disease with its own antibodies made by the white blood cells
9. A rise in blood cholesterol leading to an increased risk of heart disease
10. Central nervous system consists of brain, spinal cord and nerve cells
11. Relay, sensory and motor
12. Atherosclerosis, heart disease or high blood pressure
13. The Atkins diet
14. Because the flu virus changes regularly
15. HIV is a virus that has a high mutation rate
16. An organism that transports a pathogen from one organism to another, e.g. a mosquito
17. Phagocytes and lymphocytes
18. Natural immunity is when the body can remember a disease and produce antibodies to fight it before any symptoms develop
19. The body maintaining a constant internal environment
20. 140 years ago
21. Alleles
22. FSH, LH, oestrogen and progesterone
23. Bacteria
24. No because measles is a virus; penicillin can only kill bacteria
25. Charles Darwin
26. Lamarck
27. Antibiotics
28. Class C
29. Organic farming
30. Inside the nucleus of your cells (except red blood cells)

Chemistry
Quick test answers

Page 39 Atoms and elements
1. The nucleus
2. Elements are made of just one type of atom
3. By sharing electrons or by giving and taking electrons
4. O
5. K
6. Sodium
7. Chromium
8. It consists of hydrogen atoms and oxygen atoms in the ratio two to one
9. It consists of calcium atoms and oxygen atoms in the ratio one to one
10. It consists of sodium atoms, nitrogen atoms and oxygen atoms in the ratio one to one to three

Page 41 Limestone
1. Calcium carbonate
2. Sedimentary
3. Igneous
4. Neutralise acidity in lakes and soils
5. Zinc carbonate → zinc oxide + carbon dioxide
6. $ZnCO_{3(s)} \rightarrow ZnO_{(s)} + CO_{2(g)}$
7. Roasting clay and limestone
8. Heating limestone, sand and soda
9. Sodium carbonate, carbon dioxide and water

Page 43 Fuels
1. Coal, oil and natural gas
2. Millions of years
3. Hydrogen and carbon
4. Runny, easy to ignite and have low boiling points
5. Short ones
6. At the top

Page 45 Organic families
1. Four
2. 'Saturated' because they contain no double bonds: 'hydrocarbons' – because they contain only hydrogen and carbon atoms
3. Methane
4. [structural formulae of methane, ethane, propane, butane]
5. [structural formulae of ethene, propene]
6.
7. Alkenes decolourise bromine water while alkanes do not react
8. C_nH_{2n+2}
9. Alcohols
10. C_2H_5OH

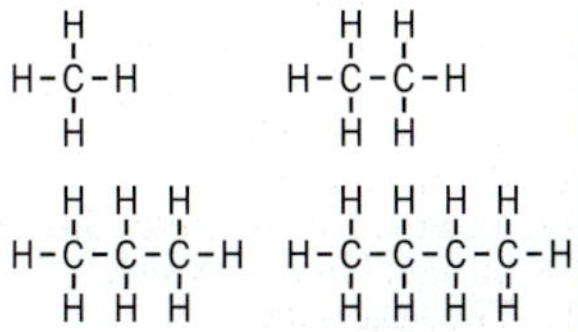

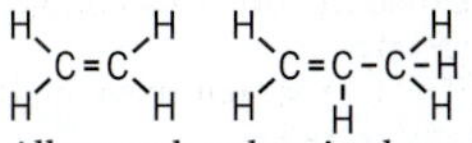

Page 47 Vegetable oils
1. Fruits, seeds and nuts
2. Seeds
3. Vitamins A and D
4. Because fats can reach much higher temperatures than water
5. Fried
6. Saturated
7. Lots of C=C bonds

Page 49 Plastics
1. [polymerisation of ethene to polythene]
2. [polymerisation of propene to polypropene]
3. Addition polymerisation
4. Monomer
5. Vinyl chloride
6. Teflon
7. Hydrogel
8. Polythene
9. Polypropene
10. Polypropene

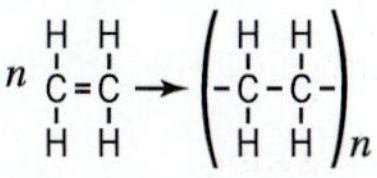

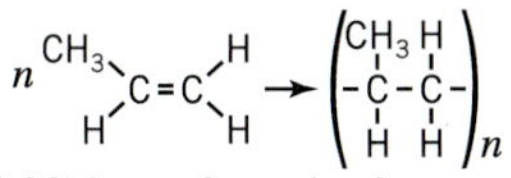

Page 51 Ethanol
1. C_2H_5OH
2. Drinks, solvents and as a fuel
3. They could become blind or even die
4. A purple dye and an unpleasant taste
5. Yeast
6. $C_6H_{12}O_6$
7. It becomes denatured
8. Phosphoric acid
9. Ethene + steam → ethanol

Page 53 Evolution of the atmosphere
1. 20%
2. Nitrogen
3. Carbon dioxide, water vapour and noble gases
4. Carbon dioxide, steam, ammonia and methane
5. Carbon dioxide
6. Removed carbon dioxide and produced oxygen
7. Became locked up in sedimentary rocks and fossil fuels
8. Filters out harmful UV rays
9. New, more complex life forms could develop
10. Burning fossil fuels

Page 55 Pollution of the atmosphere
1. Sulphur dioxide
2. Coal
3. If less electricity is required, fewer fossil fuels will need to be burnt
4. It will have a yellow colour
5. Carbon dioxide
6. Carbon monoxide
7. Smoke particles
8. A reduction in the amount of sunlight that reaches the Earth's surface, which may even affect weather patterns
9. Carbon dioxide
10. Carbon dioxide

Page 57 Pollution of the environment
1. Bauxite
2. Rainforests
3. Recycle aluminium
4. The quarries can scar the landscape
5. New jobs and brings money into the area
6. They can cause noise, congestion and damage the roads
7. Landfill sites
8. Non-biodegradable
9. Hydrogen chloride
10. Biodegradable ones

Page 59 Evidence for plate tectonics
1. Crust
2. Solid
3. Silicon, oxygen and aluminium
4. Iron and nickel
5. A few centimetres per year
6. Crust and upper mantle
7. The Earth's surface shrank as it cooled
8. Natural radioactive decay

Page 61 Consequences of plate tectonics
1. Past each other, towards each other or away from each other
2. When plates move past each other
3. There are too many factors involved
4. California, USA
5. Oceanic
6. The oceanic plate melts
7. Because plates are moving past each other
8. Iron
9. The Earth's magnetic field

Page 63 Extraction of iron
1. Gold
2. Heat with carbon
3. Electrolysis
4. Haematite
5. Iron ore, coke and limestone
6. Oxygen from hot air
7. Carbon monoxide
8. More dense
9. Slag
10. In road building and fertilisers

Page 65 Iron and steel
1. Steel
2. Water and oxygen
3. Stops water and oxygen reaching the iron
4. Magnesium or zinc
5. Hard, strong and does not rust but is brittle
6. Carbon
7. Wrought iron
8. The atoms have a very regular structure, and so the layers can pass easily over each other
9. Carbon
10. Iron, chromium and nickel

Page 67 Aluminium
1. Bauxite
2. It is soft and has a low density
3. An alloy
4. It is protected by a layer of aluminium oxide
5. Al_2O_3
6. Electrolysis
7. Oxide ions
8. Aluminium ions
9. Carbon, graphite
10. They react with oxygen to form carbon dioxide

Page 69 Titanium and copper
1. Alloy it with other metals
2. Titanium quickly reacts with oxygen to form a layer of titanium oxide, which stops any further reactions
3. To make replacement joints
4. Rutile
5. Titanium oxide or dioxide
6. $Cu^{2+} + 2e^- \rightarrow Cu$

Page 71 Transition metals
1. Free electrons
2. Middle section
3. A high melting point, high density, shiny, tough and hard wearing: they form coloured compounds and are good catalysts
4. It is a good electrical conductor that can be bent
5. It does not corrode or fracture
6. Iron is brittle
7. Bridges, buildings, ships, cars and trains
8. The Haber process
9. Coins
10. Margarine

Page 73 The noble gases
1. They have a full outer shell of electrons
2. It increases
3. [He atom diagram]
4. [Ar atom diagram]
5. Individual atoms
6. Balloons and airships
7. It is less dense than air and it is not flammable
8. Electrical discharge tubes
9. Filament light bulbs
10. Lasers

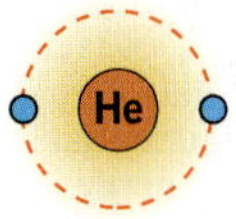

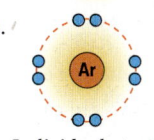

Answers to Practice questions
Page 74
1. a) Limestone/marble/chalk
   b) Calcium oxide/carbon dioxide
   c) $Ca(OH)_2$
   d) Glass
2. a) CH_4
   b) Ethane
   c) Alkanes
   d) C_2H_4
   e) Propene
   f) Alkenes
3. a) Fractional distillation
   b) More flammable
   c) Cracking
4. B
5. a) Alloy
   b) Carbon
6. In the titanium alloy the layers of atoms cannot pass easily over each other
7. C, A, D, B
8. a) Aluminium
   b) Aluminium
   c) Iron
   d) Gold

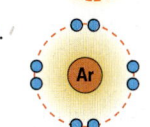

Physics
Quick test answers

Page 77 Energy
1. Heat, light, sound, electricity, chemical
2. Elastic potential energy, gravitational potential energy and chemical energy
3. Electric fire, electric bell, loudspeaker, electric motor, etc.
4. Gravitational potential energy
5. Electric hair dryer
6. It is there for our use at the flick of a switch
7. a) Television, b) Electric lawn mower or hedge trimmer, and c) Transmitting electrical energy from the power stations to your home i.e. the National Grid

Page 79 Efficiency
1. Energy may be wasted as heat energy
2. 90%
3. 70%
4. 33%
5. 30%
6. 380 J
7. To reduce our energy demand so that sources will last longer and environmental problems are addressed

Page 81 Generating electricity
1. Coal, oil and gas
2. Uranium or plutonium
3. Carbon dioxide
4. Coal and oil
5. Oil spillage
6. Cannot be replaced
7. More efficient insulation and engines and more use of alternative sources of energy
8. There are no polluting gases released and the rate at which the fossil fuels are used is reduced

Page 83 Renewable sources of energy
1. Wind and biomass
2. Wind and hydroelectric
3. a) Solar, b) Biomass (wood), c) Geothermal, d) Tidal or wind

Page 85 Heat transfer – conduction
1.

Type of insulation	Typical cost	Typical annual saving	Payback time	Rank order
Double glazing	£4000	£100	40 years	4
Cavity wall	£800	£80	10 years	3
Loft insulation	£210	£70	3 years	1
Drought excluders	£120	£30	4 years	2

Page 87 Heat transfer – convection
1. It becomes less dense
2. It becomes more dense and falls
3. Too much energy lost up the chimney
4. To prevent heat loss by convection
5. It should be at the top of the compartment
6. Hot air will rise from the beach so an onshore breeze will blow.
7. Air above the fire is warmed, becomes less dense and rises. Cooler, more dense fresh air enters the second shaft to replace the stale air.

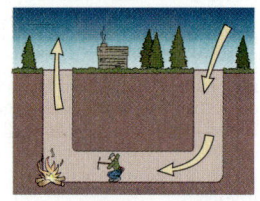

Page 89 Heat transfer – radiation
1. Electromagnetic radiation or infrared waves
2. Because conduction and convection require particles; only radiation can travel through a vacuum
3. Absorbed or reflected
4. Dark and rough
5. Light-coloured and smooth
6. A photograph taken using the radiation emitted by an object and whose colours show the temperatures of different objects
7. So that they reflect the radiation and so are cooler
8. They are both covered with ice and snow and so are white. Because they are white they reflect most of the thermal radiation from the Sun and so remain cold

Page 91 Electrical power
1. a) 6000 J, b) 150 kJ, c) 72 kJ, d) 240 kJ, e) 600 kJ
2. a) 9 units, b) 1 unit, c) 3 units, d) 2 units, e) 1 unit
3. £154

Page 93 Radiation/waves
1. a) Light waves and b) sound waves
2. Travel through vacuum, transverse

Page 95 The electromagnetic spectrum
1. Radio, microwave, visible
2. Infrared, microwaves
3. Ultraviolet, X-ray and gamma
4. Gamma
5. Visible light and infrared
6. Radioactivity
7. Microwaves can pass more easily through the Earth's atmosphere
8. There is the possibility that the X-rays may damage the foetus

Page 97 Analogue and digital signals
1. It strikes the sides at angles greater than the critical angle and so is totally internally reflected
2. Infrared and visible light
3. Cheaper, lighter, carry more signals, more secure
4. As they travel they get weaker and so must be amplified
5. Unwanted distortions that are 'picked up' by a signal as it travels
6. Noise alters the shape of an analogue signal
7. The distortions of the signal caused by the noise are amplified. The received signal may be very different from the original
8. The final signal received is a perfect copy of the original

Page 99 Radioisotopes
1. Protons and neutrons
2. Because they are unstable
3. They are atoms of an element which contain different numbers of neutrons
4. They are isotopes of an element which emit radiation
5. So that we can choose the most appropriate radiation for a particular use
6. a) gamma, b) alpha, c) beta, d) beta, e) gamma

Page 101 Radioactivity and half life
1. Rocks, e.g. granite, medical sources, from space, the air
2. Radiographer, nuclear power worker
3. Alpha
4. 3 days
5. 12 minutes

Page 103 Uses of radioactivity
1. a) beta and b) gamma
2. Tracer
3. Cell damage due to alpha radiation
4. Radiotherapy
5. Gamma
6. The creation of ions by the alpha emitter

Page 105 Our universe
1. There is a change from high frequency to lower frequency
2. It too appears to have a lower frequency
3. Red shift
4. The red shift from the very distant galaxy is greater than that of the nearer galaxy. This suggests that the further an object is from Earth the faster it is moving away from us
5. All in one place
6. It continues to expand. It stops expanding and contracts (Big Crunch). It may then explode and start to expand again (The Oscillating Universe)

Page 107 Exploring space
1. Refracting telescopes use lenses to collect light and create images. Reflecting telescopes use mirrors
2. Easier to manufacture a precise mirror, also avoids chromatic aberration
3. Galileo
4. Sir Isaac Newton
5. To avoid distortions caused by the Earth's atmosphere and avoid light pollution
6. Radio waves, microwaves, ultraviolet, infrared, X-rays and gamma rays
7. Hubble Telescope
8. The images are not affected by sunlight, cloud or rain

Answers to Practice questions
Page 108
1. a) electric lift
   b) electric motor
2. a) coal, oil and gas
   b) Once they have been used they cannot be replaced
   c) wood
   d) Use renewable sources of energy, insulate homes and factories to reduce energy wastage and develop more efficient machines and generators
3. An energy source which will not be exhausted. Wind, tidal and solar
4. 60%. Lost as heat to the surroundings
5. 3000 J
6. a) Chemical energy to heat to kinetic (turbine) to kinetic (generator) to electrical
   b) The release of carbon dioxide makes worse the greenhouse effect (global warming) and the release of sulphur dioxide increases the effects of acid rain on the environment.
7. a) gravitational potential energy
   b) kinetic energy
   c) Water is stored in the top lake until electrical energy is needed
   d) 75%
8. 6 units, 66p
9. a) 4 units
   b) 3 units
   c) 1 unit
10. 2 years, 15 years, 8 years and 3 years
11. Because they lose heat from their bodies more rapidly, they have a larger *relative* surface area
12. a) A is radio waves and B is gamma waves
    b) gamma waves have shorter wavelengths and larger frequencies
    c) microwaves and infrared waves
    d) microwaves, radio waves and visible light
13. 850 Hz
14. Microwaves
15. Cleaner signal is received, can be handled by computer
16. Radiotherapy, sterilisation and radioactive tracers (bloodstream)